CONTEMPORARY'S

GED Essay

Writing Skills to Pass the Test

Tim Collins
National-Louis University
Chicago, Illinois

Reviewers

Linda Cabose, coordinator GED Success Program
Grand Ledge Adult Ed Program
Lansing, Michigan

Carol Tharnish, GED instructor
Kankakee Community College
Kankakee, Illinois

E. Sandy Powell, ABE/GED instructor
Southwestern Oregon Community College
Gold Beach, Oregon

Development Editor: Jennifer Krasula
Executive Editor: Linda Kwil
Creative Director: Michael E. Kelly
Marketing Manager: Sean Klunder
Production Manager: Genevieve Kelley

Interior Design and Production by Think Design Group LLC

McGraw-Hill/Contemporary

A Division of The McGraw·Hill Companies

Send all inquiries to:

McGraw-Hill/Contemporary
One Prudential Plaza, Suite 400
Chicago, IL 60601

ISBN: 0-07-252758-7

Printed in the United States of America.

3 4 5 6 7 8 9 10 QPD 07 06 05 04 03

Table of Contents

Acknowledgements

Page 1: Jean-Claude LeJeune/Stock Boston

Page 29: Stephen Agricola/Stock Boston

Page 47: David Young-Wolff/PhotoEdit

Page 65: © 2001 PhotoDisc, Inc.

Page 85: © Michael J. Okoniewski/Image Works

Page 105: © Esbin/Anderson/Image Works

Page 123: © Robert Holmes/CORBIS

Page 139: Frank Siteman/Stock Boston

Page 157: Bob Daemmrich/Stock Boston

Page 177: © 2001 PhotoDisc, Inc.

Page 197: © Stephanie Maze/CORBIS

To the Student

An important part of preparing for Part II of the GED Language Arts, Writing Test is understanding what you'll be asked to do on the test. In the past, you may have completed many different kinds of writing tasks—writing a letter to apply for a job, writing directions to your home, or writing a note to a child's teacher. Each of these writing tasks required something different from you. Writing a GED essay has its own requirements, too.

Contemporary's GED Essay begins by telling you exactly what is required to write a good GED essay. In the first chapter, you will begin to analyze sample GED essay topics, understand the four-point scoring guide readers will use to score your essay, and study examples of actual GED essays.

At the end of Chapter 1 you will take a **diagnostic Pretest**. This pretest will ask you to respond to an essay topic that is similar to the topics on the GED Test. You will use the essay evaluation guidelines at the end of the pretest to determine your initial writing strengths and weaknesses. This will help you to focus on areas of improvement as you work through the rest of the book.

Writing Skills and Strategies

After you take the pretest, you will be ready to learn the skills and strategies that will help you write a good GED essay:

- A simple four-step **writing process** (Chapter 2)

- Common **essay structures**—the one-paragraph essay, the three-paragraph essay, and the five-paragraph essay (Chapters 3, 6, and 10)

- Major **types of writing** (Chapters 4, 5, 7, 8, 9, and 11), including description, process, cause and effect, narration, comparison and contrast, and persuasion

- **Revision criteria** based on the GED Essay Scoring Guide (Chapter 12)

Finally, you will complete your study with a **comprehensive review** (Chapter 13) and useful **test-taking tips** (Chapter 14). After you have worked through all the chapters in this book, you should take the **Posttest**, which will ask you to respond to a simulated GED essay topic. The Posttest will help you determine whether you are ready for Part II of the GED Language Arts, Writing Test, and, if not, which areas of the book you need to review. You can use the **Practice Test** as a final indicator of your readiness for the GED Test.

Special Features of This Book

Chapters 3–11 are organized into sections that present writing skills in the context of each chapter's theme—either a type of writing or an essay structure.

You will begin each chapter by reading and analyzing a sample essay and continue your study of the theme in four sections.

- In **Learning to Write**, you will learn more about the type of writing or essay structure used for the opening essay.

- In **Expanding Ideas**, you will learn to use a particular graphic organizer to help you gather or organize ideas for an essay.

- In **Looking at Language**, you will focus on reviewing specific areas of organization, sentence structure, usage, or mechanics.

- In **Writing a GED Essay**, you will apply what you have learned by responding to a GED-style essay topic.

In addition to this unique structure, the chapters in *Contemporary's GED Essay* contain a variety of exercises.

- **Practice exercises** cover major concepts presented in each chapter.

- **GED Connection exercises** test your understanding of organization, sentence structure, usage, and mechanics. The format of these exercises is identical to the multiple-choice format used on Part I of the Language Arts, Writing Test.

- **GED Practice exercises** give you plenty of extra practice writing GED essays.

- **Writing and Life exercises** give additional writing practice while addressing real life situations. Each topic correlates to one of the three role maps developed by the National Institute for Literacy's Equipped for the Future—Citizen/Community Member, Parent/Family, and Worker.

- **Self-Assessment exercises** give you the opportunity to assess your writing skills and develop areas for improvement.

Finally, *Contemporary's GED Essay* contains a number of features designed to make the task of test preparation more effective.

- **Additional Essay Topics** at the back of the book give you extra practice writing GED essays.

- The **Writing Handbook** contains an organized listing of the concepts presented in the *Looking at Language* sections of this book, along with a 25-question simulation of Part I of the Language Arts, Writing Test.

- The **Answer Key** explains the correct answers for the exercises.

- An **Evaluation Chart** will help you determine your readiness for Part I of the Language Arts, Writing Test.

- A **Glossary** and **Index** are included at the back of the book for easy reference.

- A copy of the **GED Essay Scoring Guide** and a **Table of Common Errors** appear on the inside-front and inside-back covers for easy reference.

The skills you acquire as you work through this book will help you when you take the Part II of the Language Arts, Writing Test and in other future writing tasks as well. Good luck on the GED Test!

CHAPTER 1

The GED Essay

An important part of the GED Test is the essay that is a part of the Language Arts, Writing Test. Often, the essay causes a lot of anxiety for test takers. However, there is no need to worry excessively. Each year hundreds of thousands of candidates obtain their GED, and all of them pass the essay test. You can too! This book contains a complete plan for developing the writing skills you need to receive a passing score and to continue your success in the workplace or at a college or university.

What do you need to do to get a passing score on the Language Arts, Writing Test? Check your knowledge by answering the following questions.

1. How much time do you have to write your GED essay?

2. Do you need special knowledge or information to write a good GED essay?

3. If you have poor spelling or handwriting, will it count against you?

4. If the reader doesn't agree with the ideas in your essay, will it affect your score?

5. Is there a length requirement for the GED essay?

6. What is the minimum passing score for the GED essay?

Don't worry if you cannot answer all of the questions. The answers can be found in the rest of the chapter.

Understanding the GED Essay Test

The GED Language Arts, Writing Test consists of two parts. Part I, Editing, is a multiple-choice test that assesses your knowledge of organization, sentence structure, usage, and mechanics. Part II, The Essay, is a test of your ability to express yourself in writing.

In Part II of the test, you will have 45 minutes to write an essay on a topic of general interest. You do not need to have any special knowledge or skills in order to write your essay. Rather, you can answer the essay question using your general knowledge. You can answer based upon your experiences as an adult. Here is a typical GED essay topic:

TOPIC

What is one important goal you would like to achieve in the next few years?

In your essay, identify that goal. Explain how you plan to achieve it. Use your personal observations, experience, and knowledge.

Reprinted with permission of the GED Testing Service.

Notice that the question does not require any specialized knowledge. You just need to be able to think of a goal you would like to achieve and explain why you want to achieve it. Other GED essay topics might ask you to explain your opinion about a common issue or the causes and effects of an everyday problem.

Notice, also, that there is no minimum number of words. Your essay simply needs to be long enough to explain your ideas adequately.

GED Essay Scores

Your score on the GED essay will represent 37 to 40 percent of your total score on the GED Language Arts, Writing Test. The remaining part of the score is from the multiple-choice portion. Each essay is scored on a scale of 1 to 4, and the minimum passing score on the essay is a 2. If your score is lower than that, you will have to take both parts of the Language Arts, Writing Test again.

Two readers trained to use holistic scoring will evaluate your completed essay. With holistic scoring, readers do not read your paper and mark each misspelled word or missing comma. Nor do they write comments about the content and structure of your writing. Rather, they read your paper and rate its overall effectiveness. The readers will consider the following features as they read your essay:

- Does the essay have well-focused main points?

- Does the essay have clear organization?

- Does the essay develop its main idea with specific details?

- Does the essay have correct sentence structure, punctuation, grammar, word choice, and spelling?

Each reader will rate your essay on a 4-point scale, with 1 (inadequate) being the lowest and 4 (effective) being the highest. Then the two readers' scores are averaged to produce a final score.

The readers are trained to evaluate your essay fairly and consistently. They are also trained to avoid unfair practices. Here are some things good readers should do:

- Good readers should not consider poor handwriting, wide or narrow margins, or writing on every other line when scoring an essay.

- Good readers should not mark spelling or grammar errors on essays. Instead, they should read with their pens down and only mark their overall holistic reaction to the paper. Poor grammar or spelling will lower a score only when it interferes with the overall effectiveness of the essay. In other words, if the grammar and spelling are so bad that the reader has trouble understanding the ideas, the score may go down. However, a few spelling or grammar errors will not lower a score.

- Good readers should not consider whether they agree with the writer's ideas or opinions. A writer may express ideas that the readers disagree with or dislike, but readers should not consider this when they score an essay. Instead, they should only consider whether the writer adequately explains the main idea of the essay and supports it with specific facts and examples.

- Good readers should not give an essay a low score because the writer only had time to write one draft. Instead, readers should keep in mind that test takers have only 45 minutes to complete their essays, and they should score the essays accordingly.

EXERCISE 1

Directions: Answer each question below.

1. How much time do you have to write your GED essay?

    _____

2. Do you need special knowledge or information to write a good GED essay?

    _____

3. If you have poor spelling or penmanship, will it count against you?

    _____

4. If the reader doesn't agree with the ideas in your essay, will it affect your score?

    _____

5. Is there a length requirement for the GED essay?

    _____

6. What is the minimum passing score for the GED essay?

    _____

Answers are on page 269.

The GED Essay Scoring Guide

The GED Essay Scoring Guide is used to help readers score GED essays. On the next page is a copy of the actual scoring guide that the readers will use.

Language Arts, Writing, Part II

Essay Scoring Guide

	1 Inadequate	2 Marginal	3 Adequate	4 Effective
Response to the Prompt	Reader has difficulty identifying or following the writer's ideas.	Reader occasionally has difficulty understanding or following the writer's ideas.	Reader understands the writer's ideas.	Reader understands and easily follows the writer's expression of ideas.
	Attempts to address the prompt but with little or no success in establishing a focus.	Addresses the prompt, though the focus may shift.	Uses the prompt to establish a main idea.	Presents a clearly focused main idea that addresses the prompt.
Organization	Fails to organize ideas.	Shows some evidence of an organizational plan.	Uses an identifiable organizational plan.	Establishes a clear and logical organization.
Development and Details	Demonstrates little or no development; usually lacks details or examples or presents irrelevant information.	Has some development but lacks specific details; may be limited to a listing, repetitions, or generalizations.	Has focused but occasionally uneven development; incorporates some specific detail.	Achieves coherent development with specific and relevant details and examples.
Conventions of EAE	Exhibits minimal or no control of sentence structure and the conventions of Edited American English (EAE).	Demonstrates inconsistent control of sentence structure and the conventions of EAE.	Generally controls sentence structure and the conventions of EAE.	Consistently controls sentence structure and the conventions of EAE.
Word Choice	Exhibits weak and/or inappropriate words.	Exhibits a narrow range of word choice, often including inappropriate selections.	Exhibits appropriate word choice.	Exhibits varied and precise word choice.

Reprinted with permission of the GED Testing Service.

How do readers apply the scoring guide to different papers? Read the following GED essays about the topic on page 2, and compare them with their scoring comments.

Essay 1

Over the next few years, my main goal is to obtain a college degree from St. Johns University in Collegville. This goal will be very difficult to obtain and I will need to work hard at it. Three things that will affect the outcome of my goal are; how much money I can raise to pay for it, how much time I am willing to spend studying, and my dedication in training for football.

Before you can register at a college, you must consider how it is going to be paid for. This is especially an issue at St. Johns, because the tuition is around $22,000 a year. This is a huge sum of money. ~~It does not make it any easier~~ It is not made easier by the fact that my parents will be able to contribute very little towards my education. Thus I am forced to rely on scholarships, grants, and loans from the government and other agencies. I have already taken some action by applying for scholarships, but I will have to apply again next year. I received a $7,500 scholarship from St. John's and they have also given me some grants. The rest of the money will have to come from student loans and an on campus job.

The next area ~~in which I will~~ that will affect my goal is the classroom. This is important because the main point of college is to prepare meself for a successful ~~care~~ career. In college, I will need to apply myself and take time to study every night. Sometimes, I may be forced to give up things that I would rather do, but I must if I am going to achieve my goal. I must create a relationship with my professors because they will ~~grade the~~ help me obtain the information that is needed to be successful.

The third thing is my dedication in training for football. Football is my favorite sport and St. Johns has an excellent football tradition. They have 150 players out for football each year. If I am going to be successful and contribute to the team, I am going to have to be dedicated to training. I ~~will~~ must spend timeless hours in the weight room gaining strength and quickness. I believe all of the hard work will pay off.

If I can do these three things, I will successfully complete my goal of graduating from college. ~~&~~ If this goal is achieved, I believe I will be well on my way to a successful life.

This essay scored a 4. Notice that it contains a clearly focused main idea (to obtain a college degree) and develops three supporting ideas to explain it. Specific examples and details about paying for college, studying effectively, and training for football help create a well-developed essay. The essay has a good command of vocabulary, and sentence structure and grammar are consistently under control. In general, the essay is clear and easy to follow.

Essay 2

I have many goals that I wish to accomplish in the next few years. The main goal, however, is that I wish to keep from incinerating my keys in molten lava.

I believe that it would be a very unfortunate thing to drop my keys in lava, considering the lava would quickly melt them. I have never met someone who has done this before, but that is probably a good thing since you'd almost have to be at an erupting volcano to be near molten lava.

To keep from doing this, I will take several precautions. First, I will stay as far away from erupting volcanos. This will not only prevent me from dropping my keys in lava, but will also help me to maintain a hope of survival. The second thing I will do is to make sure that I keep my keys in my pockets at all times in the event that I am ever close to lava. This will make it harder for my keys to come in contact with the lava, except by the chance that I fall into it, and in that case I probably won't need my keys anymore. The third thing I will do to prevent incinerating my keys in lava will be to always carry two bags with me, so that if anyone asks for a hand with something, I can say, "Sorry, I've got these two bags." I also believe that we should make the world a safer place for our children, but not our children's children, because I don't think children should be having sex.

In closing, I would like to leave one piece of very useful advice: If you ever drop your keys in a river of molten lava, forget them, they're gone.

Reprinted with permission of the GED Testing Service.

This essay scored a 3. The writer is obviously attempting to be humorous, which may or may not appeal to some readers, but the essay does present an adequate response. It has a definite main idea ("I wish to keep from incinerating my keys in molten lava"), and the writer develops that idea with a focused paragraph of precautionary steps. Sentence structure, grammar, and spelling are under control, and word choice is appropriate.

Essay 3

An important goal I would like to achieve in the next few years, is to settle down on the kind of life style I'm living. Running around ~~witt~~ like I have no responsibilities when I actually do. I think I can achieve this goal in a few ways. 1) The first thing I must do is get a steady job that I at least halfway enjoy & Stick with that co. or coorporation until I can move up in the world. Then I'm going try to settle down even more and try to find ~~find~~ a family. If that happens then give my children the best life I've never had. With what I know about a hard life I'll never want my children to ever know. Theres not alot to say about my goal except I know doing this is probably going to be the hardest thing I've ever done in my entire life. Alot of my experiences with moving into the "real world" have gone sour, that's why I understand just how hard it really is and is going to be.

Reprinted with permission of the GED Testing Service.

This essay scored a 2. The writer addresses the topic, but the organization is limited to one paragraph. There is some development of the idea that the writer would like to achieve the goal of settling down, but the response lacks specific details and remains on a general level throughout. There are errors in grammar, spelling, and sentence structure that interfere with the reader's ability to understand the writer's ideas.

Essay 4

The only goal I have is to see that my girlfriend and I get married and a healthy baby. It gets hard from time to time bet we've always managed to get over or through it. She's all ready pregnant but I do every thing I can so that the baby will be has healthy as it can be. I now it will be hard to do but I am willing to take all responable and take care of her and my child. I think that this is the best goal I have in my life because her and that little bundle of joy in side of her mean more to me than any thing in this hole world.

Reprinted with permission of the GED Testing Service.

This essay scored a 1. Notice that there is an attempt to address the topic ("to see that my girlfriend and I get married and a healthy baby"), but there is little or no development. The writer gives few details except the admission that achieving the goal will be difficult. There is little control of grammar, spelling, or sentence structure, which makes the essay hard to understand.

EXERCISE 2

Directions: Look at the following GED topic and sample essays. Use the GED Essay Scoring Guide on page 5 to score the essays.

———————————————————— T O P I C ————————————

Who is your best friend? What makes that person special?

In your essay, identify your best friend and tell why you are such good friends. Use your personal observations, experience, and knowledge.

Essay 1   Score: _____

My best friend Stacy. She ~~is~~ my best friend because she very cool. We go everyplace togeter and have fun. Last year Stacy had a baby, so now she busy a lot and I miss her. But we talk on the phone.

Essay 2   Score: _____

My best friend is Gerardo. He is a good friend because we have the same values and intrests.

I like gerardo cuz he has really good values. He works hard at his job as a community activist. He works for an agency that help victims of domestic abuse. He is always goin to meetings to combat violence against ~~wr~~ kids from their parents. He also organize a rally to stop street crime.

Gerardo and me have many similar interests. ~~He likes to~~ We like to work on our cars and to take pictures with our cameras. We both have nice cameras, and we spend a lot of time together taking pictures.

Essay 3   Score: _____

My best friend is my wife, Daisy. Daisy is a good friend because we always get along and never fight or disagree. Daisy is very intelligent too and I like that. She is the one who said, "Go back and Get Your GED," so I did and look at me—I hope to pass all the tests soon. I like to spend time with her, too. Last ~~year~~ month we went to several flower and plant shows to buy plants for our garden. Then we worked together to plant & water them. But now the garden looks ~~pret~~ grate. I wish that all my friends had a wife as nice as Daisy. This is why she is not only a wife but also a best friend.

Answers are on page 269.

Language Arts, Writing, Part II

Essay Directions and Topic:

Look at the box on the following page. In the box is your assigned topic. You must write on the assigned topic ONLY.

You will have 45 minutes to write on your assigned essay topic. If you run out of time, mark where you were in your essay. Then complete the essay. This will help you determine how much faster you need to work to complete your essay in 45 minutes.

Pay attention to the following features as you write:

- Well-focused main points

- Clear organization

- Specific development of your ideas

- Control of sentence structure, punctuation, grammar, word choice, and spelling

As you work, be sure to do the following:

- Write legibly **in ink.**

- Write on the assigned topic.

- Write your essay on a separate sheet of paper.

PRETEST

What is the most interesting trip you ever took?

In your essay, identify that trip. Explain why it was memorable. Use your personal observations, experience, and knowledge.

This Pretest will help you determine how well you can use written language to explain your ideas.

In preparing your essay, you should take the following steps:

- Read the **DIRECTIONS** and the **TOPIC** carefully.

- Plan your essay before you write. Use scratch paper to make any notes.

- After you finish writing your essay, reread what you have written and make any changes that will improve your essay.

Your essay should be long enough to develop the topic adequately.

Evaluation guidelines are on page 14.

Evaluation Guidelines

If possible ask your instructor or another student to give your essay an overall score using the GED Essay Scoring Guide. If you need to score your paper yourself, let your paper sit for a few days and then score it.

Write your score here: _____

Now look at the GED Essay Scoring Guide on page 5 or on the inside front cover of this book.

Score your essay according to each area of the scoring guide. Then write the score for each area in the second column of the chart below. For each score of 2 or below, pay attention to the instructions in column 3.

Area	Score	Instruction
Response to Prompt		Pay attention to the *Learning to Write* sections in this book.
Organization		Pay attention to the *Expanding Ideas* sections in this book.
Development and Details		Pay attention to the *Expanding Ideas* sections in this book.
Conventions of EAE (Edited American English)		Pay attention to the *Looking at Language* sections in this book.
Word Choice		Pay attention to the *Looking at Language* sections in this book.

CHAPTER 2

The Writing Process

Forty-five minutes is plenty of time to write a GED essay when you have a plan. Read the GED essay topic and sample essays below. Which essay do you think received a higher score?

TOPIC

People have different motivations for getting their GED. What is your motivation?

In your essay, explain why you want to get your GED. Give specific examples to back up your reasons. Use your personal observations, experience, and knowledge.

Essay 1

My brother get his GED last year, and now he has a good job. I needs a good job, too. I left high school when I was a freshman and never went back. If I get a GED my kids will look up to me. If I get a better job I will make more money. I need money to move to a bigger apartment because my kids are getting older and need more room.

Essay 2

Getting a GED will make my life better in several ways. First, with a GED I can get a better job. At my company, you need a GED or high school diploma to get a job as a telephone representative. If I get a job as a telephone representative, I can move out of my job in the warehouse and get more money answering customer calls. Second, getting a GED makes people feel good about themselves. I have always felt bad about leaving high school, and now I will know that I can finish. Third, my kids will look up to me more. Right now, it's hard for them to feel proud of me because I lack the education their friends' fathers have. Last, with a GED I will be able to get more education. I have always wanted to go to college, and with my GED, that dream can become a reality. So, there are many reasons why I am working so hard every night to get ready for the GED test.

Answer the following questions:

1. Which essay probably received a higher score? Why do you think so?

2. The writer of Essay 2 had a plan for writing. What kinds of steps do you think were in the writer's plan?

Overview of the Writing Process

The **writing process** is a simple plan you can use to write a good essay in the time allotted. There are four steps in the writing process:

- Gathering ideas
- Organizing
- Writing
- Revising

Gathering Ideas

This is a thinking stage. When **gathering ideas**, you examine the topic and think of ideas for your essay. If this seems difficult, relax: All GED essay questions can be answered using everyday life experiences. GED essay topics will address questions such as your favorite foods, pastimes, and activities. You may be asked to discuss your values or your experiences growing up, working, or being a parent or child. You may be asked to talk about your family, your friends, or your daily routine.

When you begin this stage of the writing process, you should examine the topic carefully and figure out your **main idea**—the point of view your essay will discuss or develop. Look at the following essay topic. What might the writer's main idea be? Write it on the line below.

--- **TOPIC** ---

Everyone has a favorite food. What is yours?

In your essay, describe your favorite food. Explain why you like it. Use your personal observations, experience, and knowledge.

Main idea: _____

What did you write? One writer decided that her favorite food is ice cream. Here is what she wrote:

Main idea: *My favorite food is ice cream.*

EXERCISE 1

Directions: Read the following GED essay topics. Write a main idea for each topic on the line below.

1.

─────────── T O P I C ───────────

Some people like large families, while others think that smaller families are better. What is your preference?

In your essay, state which size family you think is ideal. Explain your beliefs. Use your personal observations, experience, and knowledge.

Main Idea: _____

2.

─────────── T O P I C ───────────

Many medical experts think people need to get more exercise. What are the benefits of regular exercise?

In your essay, state the benefits of regular exercise. Give explanations to back up your opinion. Use your personal observations, experience, and knowledge.

Main Idea: _____

3.

─────────── T O P I C ───────────

Advances in technology have led to the wide availability of portable communication devices, such as cell phones, electronic organizers, and the wireless Internet.

Write an essay explaining how portable communication devices have affected our society.

Main Idea: _____

Answers are on page 269.

After you have figured out your main idea, you are ready to start thinking of ideas to back it up. In this book you will learn a number of tools to help you gather ideas. One of these tools is an **idea circle**. In an idea circle you write the main idea in a circle in the center of your paper. Then write supporting ideas on spokes coming from the center of the circle. As you gather ideas, try to work quickly. Use your personal observations, experience, and knowledge to help you think of ideas. Do not worry about organizing your ideas, spelling words correctly, or writing complete sentences. You will take care of these things in later steps. For now, concentrate on getting your ideas down on paper.

Here is an idea circle created for a paragraph about ice cream:

It is refreshing on a hot day.

It is sweet and cold

My favorite food is ice cream.

There are many delicious flavors.

Mint chocolate chip is my favorite flavor.

Popsicles are good too.

Notice that the writer simply jotted down a few specific ideas to use in the paragraph.

EXERCISE 2

Directions: Use the idea circle below to gather ideas for an essay on your favorite food. Write your main idea from page 16 in the circle. Then write specific supporting details on the spokes.

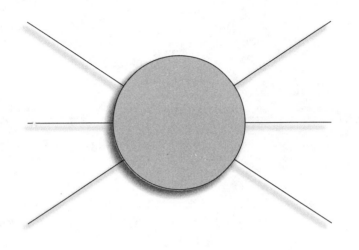

Answers are on page 269.

Organizing

In the second stage of the writing process, **organizing**, a good writer does three things:

1. Makes sure all the ideas are relevant

2. Makes sure there are enough ideas

3. Arranges the ideas in a logical order

Look again at the idea circle on ice cream (page 18). Which idea is not about the topic? Cross it off.

If you crossed off *Popsicles are good too*, you are correct. Popsicles are not a type of ice cream, so they are not relevant.

A good paragraph needs about three to four supporting sentences. Right now there are only three good ideas in the idea circle. What else might the writer add to the idea circle? Add an idea to the empty spoke.

Finally, a writer arranges the ideas in a logical order. The writer of the essay on ice cream decided to put them in order from least important to most important. Notice how she has numbered the ideas:

④ It is refreshing on a hot day.

① It is sweet and cold

My favorite food is ice cream.

② There are many different flavors.

③ Mint chocolate chip is my favorite flavor.

Popsicles ~~are~~ good too.

Arranging ideas from most important to least important is just one pattern of organization. In the following chapters of this book, you will examine several different ways to organize ideas.

EXERCISE 3

Directions: Look at the idea circle you created in Exercise 2. Make sure all of the ideas are relevant. Cross off any ideas that are not relevant. Make sure you have at least three to four good supporting ideas. Then number your ideas in a logical order.

Answers are on page 269.

Writing

When a writer begins **writing**, he or she uses the organized ideas to write sentences and paragraphs. Look at the paragraph the writer wrote about ice cream:

> My very favorite food is ice cream. I love it because it is sweet and cold. It comes in many delisious flavors. I think mint chocolate chip the best. Ice cream is really refreshing on a hot Summer day.

You may have noticed a few mistakes in the paragraph. This is nothing to worry about. The writer will take care of these mistakes in the final step.

EXERCISE 4

Directions: Use the ideas from your organized idea circle on page 19 to write a paragraph about your favorite food.

_____

_____

_____

_____

_____

_____

_____

_____

_____

_____

Answers are on page 269.

Revising

In the fourth stage of the writing process, **revising**, good writers check their work in two ways. First they make sure that their ideas are clear, complete, and relevant to the main idea. Then they also check the language. They make sure that the sentences are complete, the words are spelled correctly, and there are no other mistakes. Look back at the paragraph on ice cream (page 21). Can you find one or two errors? Circle them.

Now look at the writer's revised paragraph. Look at how she improved the final product.

> *My very favorite food is ice cream. I love it because it is sweet and cold. It comes in many delicious flavors. I think mint chocolate chip is the best. I love butter pecan, too. Ice cream is really refreshing on a hot summer day.*

The writer corrected problems with capitalization, spelling, and a missing verb. She also added an additional idea to make the paragraph longer. As you can see, the completed paragraph is much stronger.

Each of the following chapters in this book contain information about different conventions of Edited American English and will help you improve your writing.

EXERCISE 5

Directions: Look back at your paragraph on a favorite food (page 21). Check elements of grammar and content, such as sentence structure, spelling, capitalization, and punctuation. Write in your corrections.

Answers are on page 269.

EXERCISE 6

Directions: What is the order of the steps in the writing process? Write numbers from 1 (first) to 4 (last) on the appropriate lines.

_____ Organizing

_____ Writing

_____ Revising

_____ Gathering ideas

Answers are on page 269.

EXERCISE 7

Directions: What do you do in each step of the writing process? Write the name of each step from Exercise 6 on the appropriate line.

1. _____ You think of good ideas for your essay.

2. _____ You check the grammar, punctuation, and spelling.

3. _____ You arrange the ideas in order.

4. _____ You think of the main idea of your essay.

5. _____ You check the ideas you gathered to make sure they are relevant.

6. _____ You write your essay in sentences and paragraphs.

7. _____ You make sure you gathered enough ideas.

8. _____ You check your essay to make sure all of the ideas are clear, complete, and relevant.

WRITING A GED ESSAY: *The Writing Process*

- Forty-five minutes is plenty of time to write a GED essay when you have a plan.

- Good writers follow four stages when writing: gathering ideas, organizing, writing, and revising.

- After a main idea is selected, several supporting ideas should be gathered.

- An idea circle is one good way to gather ideas.

- After the ideas are gathered, they should be checked to see if there are enough supporting ideas, whether all the ideas are relevant, and whether the ideas are arranged in a logical order.

- Once the ideas are organized, the writer is ready to write the essay. The essay consists of sentences and paragraphs. At this stage it is not important to worry too much about issues such as grammar, spelling, and punctuation.

- Finally, the essay should be revised so the ideas are complete, clear, and relevant. At this stage, the language, grammar, spelling, and punctuation should be checked.

GED Practice

Directions: Use the four steps of the writing process to create a one-paragraph essay that responds to the following GED essay topic. Follow the steps below.

──────────── **T O P I C** ────────────

People have different motivation for getting their GED. What is your motivation?

In your essay, explain why you want to get your GED. Give specific examples to back your reasons. Use your personal observations, experience, and knowledge.

1. Gather Ideas

Read the essay topic and think of the main idea for your one-paragraph essay. Write your main idea in the large circle in the center of the idea circle on the next page. Then add supporting ideas to the spokes.

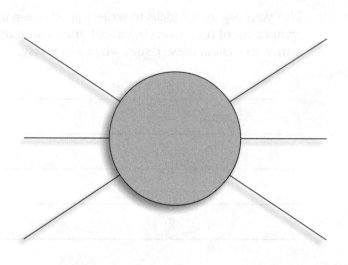

2. **Organize Your Ideas**

    A. Review your idea circle. Use the following checklist.

        ☐ My ideas are relevant.

        ☐ There are at least three to four good ideas.

    B. Decide the order you will use to write your essay. Number the ideas in this order. Cross off any ideas that are not relevant.

3. Write Your Essay

Use your organized ideas to write a good one-paragraph essay. Do not spend a lot of time worrying about grammar, punctuation, or spelling. You will worry about these issues when you revise.

_____

_____

_____

_____

_____

_____

_____

_____

_____

_____

_____

_____

_____

4. Revise Your Essay

A. Check your essay's ideas. Use the following checklist.

☐ My essay gives specific details.

☐ The ideas are clear, complete, and relevant.

B. Check your essay for standards of Edited American English. Use the following checklist.

☐ My essay uses capitalization correctly.

☐ The words are spelled correctly.

Answers are on page 269.

Writing and Life

Directions: Use the four steps of the writing process to create a one-paragraph essay that responds to the following GED essay topic.

───────────── **TOPIC** ─────────────

Today our workplaces and neighborhoods are composed of people of diverse backgrounds. For this reason it is important for people to find ways to get along with each other.

Write an essay explaining how people of diverse backgrounds can get along better.

_____

_____

_____

_____

_____

_____

_____

_____

_____

_____

_____

_____

_____

_____

_____

_____

Answers are on page 269.

Self-Assessment

Part A

Directions: Ask your instructor or a friend to review your work on page 27, or you can review it yourself. Answer the following questions. Write **yes** or **no** on the appropriate lines below.

1. _____ Does the essay have a main idea?

2. _____ Was an idea circle used to gather ideas?

3. _____ Are the ideas relevant?

4. _____ Are there enough ideas?

5. _____ Are the ideas arranged in a logical order?

6. _____ Were the gathered ideas used in the essay?

7. _____ Were the essay's ideas checked to make sure they are complete, clear, and relevant?

8. _____ Was the essay checked for correct capitalization and spelling?

Part B

Directions: Based on your answers to Part A, complete the following statements.

1. Name a new strength in your writing that you want to continue to use in future assignments.

   _____

2. Name a feature of your writing that you want to improve by reviewing the information in Chapter 2.

   _____

Answers are on page 269.

CHAPTER 3

The One-Paragraph Essay

The simplest essay consists of a single paragraph. Read the essay topic and one-paragraph essay below.

--- **T O P I C** ---

Most people like to have fun during their free time. What is your favorite free-time activity?

In your essay, state your favorite free-time activity. Explain why you like it. Use your personal observations, experience, and knowledge.

My favorite free-time activity is going out with my husband. We both have busy schedules and spend a lot of free time with our kids. But it's important for us to spend time together—just the two of us. So once or twice a month we ask my mother to baby-sit, and we go out together. Sometimes we see a movie or go out for dinner. Once in a while, we visit another couple or go to a restaurant with them. Other times, we go shopping or take a relaxing drive. No matter what we do, we always talk, laugh, and have fun. Afterwards, we are relaxed and ready to return to the challenges of our home, our kids, and our jobs.

Answer the following questions:

1. What is the writer's favorite free-time activity?

2. What kinds of things do the writer and her husband do together?

3. What are the results of the time they spend together?

4. What is your favorite activity?

LEARNING TO WRITE: *A One-Paragraph Essay*

An essay can be one or more paragraphs long. Usually, a good GED essay has several paragraphs. However, since you may be new to writing essays, the one-paragraph essay is a good place to start. In this chapter you will study and practice one-paragraph essays. In later chapters you will learn how to write multi-paragraph essays.

A **one-paragraph essay** has a very specific structure. The three parts of a good one-paragraph essay are:

1. A topic sentence

2. A number of supporting sentences

3. A concluding sentence

The Topic Sentence

The **topic sentence** states the main idea of the one-paragraph essay. A good topic sentence is usually general, not specific. For example, which of the following sentences would make a good topic sentence for an essay about someone's favorite pastime?

I love to sing in my choir.

We have fun learning new songs.

If you said the first sentence would make a good topic sentence, you are right. It is a general statement about someone's favorite pastime.

EXERCISE 1

Directions: Read the following paragraphs. Write a topic sentence for each on the appropriate line.

1. _____

My brother and his wife live in California. He is in the military, and she works in a supermarket. They have two beautiful children, Tonya and Darnell. They live in a nice apartment near the ocean. They want to buy a home near a good school next year.

2. _____

We get up early and drive to the state park. We find a secluded campsite and pitch our tent. Then we hike, fish, or visit with other campers. At night we build a fire, cook dinner, and tell stories. We always come home feeling relaxed and refreshed. We get plenty of fresh air, exercise, and sunshine.

3. _____

Every afternoon after work, I drive to the park district pool, change into my swimsuit, and dive into the cool water. I swim back and forth for about a half-hour. Then, when I am feeling relaxed, I climb out of the pool, get dressed, and drive to the daycare center to pick up my kids.

4. _____

On Sunday, my family always has a big meal together. We gather at my house about 1:00 P.M. I usually spend part of Saturday getting ready. On Sunday I start cooking about noon. By 2:00 P.M. everything is ready and all of us—my kids, my husband, and a few of my grandchildren—sit down to enjoy the meal. Sometimes my youngest son, who lives in another state, calls on the speaker phone to talk to us.

Answers are on page 270.

Supporting Sentences

Look at the sentences again:

I love to sing in my choir.

We have fun learning new songs.

The second sentence is a good example of a **supporting sentence**. A good supporting sentence states specific reasons to back up or explain the topic sentence. Notice how this sentence gives one reason why singing in a choir is the writer's favorite activity.

Good supporting sentences contain details or reasons. Supporting sentences can also provide specific examples. Look at the following examples of good supporting sentences. Can you add another supporting sentence of your own? Write it on the line below.

After rehearsal a few of us usually go out for a cup of coffee or a snack.

Our favorite song is "The Long and Winding Road." We sing it during every rehearsal and performance.

Our most exciting concert was played on public TV last year.

_____

EXERCISE 2

Directions: Look again at the paragraphs in Exercise 1. Write one more supporting sentence for each one.

1. _____

2. _____

3. _____

4. _____

Answers are on page 270.

Concluding Sentence

The **concluding sentence** sums up the paragraph. It is usually more general than the supporting sentences. It gives the reader a final idea about the topic. Look at the concluding sentence for the paragraph on singing in a choir:

> For these reasons our rehearsals and performances are the highlights of my week.

Notice how this sentence pulls together all the ideas in the essay and restates the main idea: the writer loves singing in a choir.

A good writer always writes a paragraph a certain way. He or she indents the first line to show that a new paragraph is beginning. (To **indent**, you begin the first word of the paragraph a few spaces to the right of the margin.) Look at the following example:

> ᴵⁿᵈᵉⁿᵗ I love to sing in my choir. Our rehearsals and concerts are always fun. Our favorite song is "The Long and Winding Road." We sing it during every rehearsal and performance. We have fun learning new songs. After rehearsal a few of us usually go out for a cup of coffee or a snack. Our most exciting concert was played on public TV last year. For these reasons, our rehearsals and performances are the highlights of my week.

EXERCISE 3

Directions: Reread the paragraphs in Exercise 1. Then select the best concluding sentence for each one. Check the appropriate box.

1. ☐ I am really happy for my brother and his family.
   ☐ They have a cute dog named Samantha.

2. ☐ We love to watch the stars late at night.
   ☐ When we get home, we feel invigorated and refreshed.

3. ☐ After my swim break, I am ready to spend time with my kids.
   ☐ Sometimes, I will practice diving.

4. ☐ My family and I love our special time together.
   ☐ My sister often brings two of her special pies for dessert.

Answers are on page 270.

EXERCISE 4

Directions: Reread the paragraph on page 29 and respond to the following statements.

1. Find the topic sentence of the paragraph and circle it.

2. Count the number of supporting sentences.
   Write the number of supporting sentences on the line. _____

3. Think of another possible supporting sentence. Write it on the line.

   _____

4. Find the concluding sentence. Underline it.

EXPANDING IDEAS: *Idea Lists*

An **idea list** is an easy way to gather ideas for a one-paragraph essay. To make an idea list, first write the topic of your essay at the top of the page. Underline it. Under that, write as many ideas as you can. Do not worry about whether you are spelling your ideas correctly or whether they are about the topic. As you learned in Chapter 2, you can take care of those issues later in the writing process.

Here is an example of a list that one GED candidate gathered:

My favorite activity—going out with my husband

we're always busy with work and kids—
need time together

laugh, talk

go out together

see a movie

go out to dinner

visit another couple

have dinner with another couple

sometimes we both have to work on Sundays,
so my mother has to baby-sit

go shopping

have fun

mother baby-sits

afterwards, we feel ready to deal with work
and kids again

Notice that the ideas are not in any certain order. The writer just wrote them down in the order in which she thought of them. At least one of the ideas in the list was not relevant, and she did not use it in the completed paragraph. Can you find this idea and cross if off?

If you crossed off *sometimes we both have to work on Sundays, so my mother has to baby-sit,* you are correct. Though this idea shows that they are busy parents, it does not support the main idea that her favorite activity is going out with her husband.

EXERCISE 5

Part A

Directions: Read the essay topic below. Then use an idea list to gather ideas for a one-paragraph essay.

——————————— T O P I C ———————————

Everyone has chores to do every day. What chore do you like best?

In your essay, state your favorite chore. Explain why you like it. Use your personal observations, experience, and knowledge.

_____

_____

_____

_____

_____

_____

_____

_____

_____

_____

_____

Part B

Directions: Review your idea list. Make sure your ideas are specific and relevant. Use the following checklist. Add more information to your list and cross off ideas that you can replace with stronger ones.

1. ☐ My idea list begins with a general statement of the main idea.

2. ☐ My idea list contains a number of specific ideas.

3. ☐ All of the specific ideas support or back up the main idea.

Answers are on page 270.

When you write a one-paragraph essay, the general statement of the main idea will help you write a topic sentence. The specific ideas will help you write supporting sentences. Look at the following examples:

Idea List:	My favorite activity—going out with my husband
Topic Sentence:	My favorite free-time activity is going out with my husband.
Idea List:	Go out together, mother baby-sits
Supporting Sentence:	So once or twice a month we ask my mother to baby-sit, and we go out together.

Notice that the writer combined two different ideas into one supporting sentence. This is a good way to show how your ideas are related.

EXERCISE 6

Directions: Use your idea list in Exercise 5 to answer the following questions.

1. Write the main idea from your idea list. Use it to write a topic sentence for a one-paragraph essay.

    Idea List: _____

    Topic Sentence: _____

    _____

2. Write one of the supporting ideas from your idea list. Use it to write a supporting sentence that backs up the topic sentence of a one-paragraph essay.

    Idea List: _____

    Supporting Sentence: _____

    _____

LOOKING AT LANGUAGE: *Sentence Basics*

Subjects and Verbs

The **subject** of a sentence tells *who* or *what* the sentence is about. The **verb** tells what the subject *is* or *does*. Look at the examples below. The subjects are underlined once, the verbs twice.

<u>Mr. Smith</u> <u>is</u> an excellent fisherman.

Last week <u>he</u> <u>caught</u> ten trout.

EXERCISE 7

Directions: Underline the subjects once and the verbs twice.

1. Mary Jane collects model cars and trucks.

2. She has more than 100 models in her collection.

3. She paints all of the models herself.

4. Her most valuable model is a Model T.

5. Her newest model is a PT Cruiser.

6. However, Mary Jane does not own a real car herself.

7. A car is too expensive in the city.

8. So she always takes the bus.

9. She also walks a lot too.

10. Last year she rented a car for her vacation.

Answers are on page 270.

Complete Sentences

A **complete sentence** has a subject and a verb. A sentence that lacks a subject or a verb is called a **fragment**. Look at the following examples. Which one is a complete sentence?

My husband and I to the movies almost every weekend.

My mother baby-sits for us.

If you said that *My mother baby-sits for us* is a complete sentence, you are correct. The subject is *mother* and the verb is *baby-sits*.

Can you figure out what is wrong with the first example? If you said that it needs a verb, you are correct. The sentence already has a subject—*my husband and I*. Here is a correct version of the sentence with a verb:

My husband and I **go** to the movies almost every weekend.

EXERCISE 8

Part A

Directions: Read each group of words below. On the line next to it, write **S** if the item is a sentence or **F** if the item is a fragment.

1. _____ My favorite pastime playing basketball.

2. _____ My friends and I play almost every afternoon.

3. _____ In winter play at Hill Park Gym.

4. _____ That gym has several basketball courts.

5. _____ We like to play outdoors at Lakefront Park in summer.

6. _____ About eight people every day.

7. _____ I haven't played this week.

8. _____ Hurt my leg at work, so I have been resting.

9. _____ I hope to start playing again next week when my leg is better.

10. _____ Can't wait to get back to our games!

Part B

Directions: Reread the groups of words in Part A that are not complete sentences. Add a subject or a verb to each and write complete sentences on the lines below.

1. _____

2. _____

3. _____

4. _____

5. _____

Answers are on page 270.

Capital Letters

Always begin a sentence with a capital letter.

She really enjoys working on her car.

Always write the pronoun *I* with a capital letter.

Joe and **I** like to watch TV late at night.

Use capital letters for proper nouns and adjectives. A **proper noun** is the name of a specific person, place, or thing. A **proper adjective** is an adjective formed from a proper noun, like *Mexican*.

I think that **Tyrice** wants to travel to **Mexico** some day.

She loves to eat **Mexican** food.

EXERCISE 9

Directions: Write capital letters where needed in the following sentences.

1. i went to los angeles last week to visit my sister laura and her husband, vince.

2. we had a lot of fun visiting disneyland and seeing the ocean.

3. the pacific ocean is really beautiful.

4. we went swimming at santa monica beach and drove along the coast to santa barbara.

5. for new year's eve, laura and vince are going to visit my husband and me in chicago.

Answers are on page 270.

End Punctuation

Every sentence should end with a question mark, exclamation point, or period.

End every question with a question mark.

What is your favorite pastime**?**

Do you sing in a choir**?**

An **exclamation** shows great interest or emotion. Use an exclamation point to end an exclamation.

It costs $100**!**

What a great movie**!**

Use a period to end sentences that are not questions or exclamations. Use periods in abbreviations too.

Her name is Dr. Christine Johnson.

EXERCISE 10

Directions: Use a period, question mark, or exclamation point to end each sentence below.

1. My favorite pastime is cooking

2. I love preparing meals for my family and friends

3. Of course, I work, so I don't have much time to cook on weekdays

4. That's too bad

5. But on weekends I can really enjoy myself in the kitchen

6. What kinds of things do you make

7. Well, last weekend, I made fried chicken and mashed potatoes

8. That sounds delicious

9. Are pies easy to make

10. The filling is easy, but the crust is hard

11. What's in the crust

12. Flour, shortening, and salt are in the crust

Answers are on page 270.

GED Connection

Directions: Choose the <u>one best answer</u> to each question.

(A)

(1) My favorite pastime is spending time with my dog, Emma. (2) Emma a prize-winning Labrador Retriever. (3) Emma is a great dog? (4) I stay busy looking after her. (5) First, I have to feed her every day and take her for walks. (6) She loves to run, so every day we go to memorial Park for a run. (7) This park has a special area for dogs without leashes. (8) She runs and runs, while I watch. (9) Every day I have to brush her fur, and I have to give her a bath at least once a week. (10) I also have to spend time training her. (11) On weekends, we often have to travel to dog shows. (12) Taking care of a dog like Emma is a lot of work, but I enjoy it.

1. **Sentence 2: Emma a prize-winning Labrador Retriever.**

   What correction should be made to sentence 2?

   (1) change *Labrador* to *labrador*
   (2) insert the word *is* after *Emma*
   (3) change the period to a question mark
   (4) change the period to an exclamation point
   (5) no correction is necessary

2. **Sentence 3: Emma's a great dog?**

   What correction should be made to sentence 3?

   (1) change *Emma is* to *Emma's*
   (2) insert a comma after *is*
   (3) insert the word *not* after *is*
   (4) change the question mark to an exclamation point
   (5) no correction is necessary

3. **Sentence 6: She loves to run, so every day we go to memorial Park for a run.**

   What correction should be made to sentence 6?

   (1) change *loves* to *love*
   (2) change *we* to *I*
   (3) change *memorial* to *Memorial*
   (4) change the period to a question mark
   (5) no correction is necessary

Answers are on page **271.**

WRITING A GED ESSAY: The One-Paragraph Essay

- The simplest essay consists of a single paragraph.

- A one-paragraph essay has a general topic sentence that states the main idea of the essay and several supporting sentences that list specific ideas to back up the topic sentence.

- The first line of a paragraph should always be indented.

- An idea list is a good way to gather ideas for an essay.

- Each sentence should be complete. A complete sentence has a subject and a verb.

- The first letter of a sentence should be capitalized, and it should end with a period, question mark, or exclamation point.

- Proper nouns and proper adjectives must be capitalized.

GED Practice

Directions: Use the four steps of the writing process to create a one-paragraph essay that responds to the following GED essay topic. Follow the steps below.

────────── **T O P I C** ──────────

Most people like to have fun during their free time. What is your favorite free-time activity?

In your essay, state your favorite free-time activity. Explain why you like it. Use your personal observations, experience, and knowledge.

1. Gather Ideas

Read the essay topic and think of the main idea for your one-paragraph essay. Then create an idea list to gather ideas. Write your main idea on the top line below and underline it. Then write as many ideas as you can think of under it. Use a separate sheet of paper if you need more room.

_____

_____

_____

_____

2. Organize Your Ideas

A. Review your idea list. Be sure your ideas are specific and relevant. Use the following checklist. Add more information to your idea list, and cross off ideas you can replace with stronger ideas.

    1. ☐ My idea list begins with a general statement of the main idea.

    2. ☐ My idea list contains a number of specific ideas.

    3. ☐ All of the specific ideas support or back up the main idea.

B. Decide the order you will use to write your essay. Number the ideas in this order. Cross off any ideas that are not relevant.

3. Write Your Essay

Use your organized idea list to write a good one-paragraph essay. Use the main idea to write the topic sentence. Use the supporting ideas to write supporting sentences. Do not spend a lot of time worrying about grammar, punctuation, or spelling. You will check for mistakes after you write your essay.

_____

_____

_____

_____

_____

_____

_____

_____

_____

_____

_____

_____

_____

_____

_____

_____

_____

_____

_____

_____

_____

_____

_____

_____

_____

_____

_____

_____

4. **Revise Your Essay**

    A. Check your essay's ideas using the following list.

        1. ☐ My essay begins with a topic sentence that clearly states the main idea.

        2. ☐ My supporting sentences give specific details.

        3. ☐ The specific details back up or support the topic sentence.

        4. ☐ My essay ends with a concluding sentence that sums up the paragraph.

    B. Check your essay for standards of Edited American English.

        1. ☐ The first line of my essay is indented.

        2. ☐ All of my sentences are complete.

        3. ☐ My sentences begin with a capital letter and end with a period, question mark, or exclamation point.

        4. ☐ All proper nouns and proper adjectives are capitalized.

Answers are on page 271.

Writing and Life

Directions: Use the four steps of the writing process to create a one-paragraph essay that responds to the following essay topic.

──────────── T O P I C ────────────

What is the best job you have ever had?

In your essay, state the best job you have ever had. Explain why you liked it. Use your personal observations, experience, and knowledge.

───

_____

_____

_____

_____

_____

_____

_____

_____

_____

_____

_____

_____

_____

_____

_____

_____

Answers are on page 271.

Self-Assessment

Part A

Directions: Ask your instructor or a friend to review your work on page 45, or review it yourself. Answer the following questions. Write **yes** or **no** on the appropriate lines below.

1. _____ Is the first line of the essay indented?

2. _____ Does the essay have a clear topic sentence and several supporting sentences?

3. _____ Is the topic sentence general and are the supporting sentences specific?

4. _____ Do the supporting sentences back up the topic sentence?

5. _____ Are the sentences complete, and do they begin with a capital letter and end with a period, question mark, or exclamation point?

6. _____ Are proper nouns and adjectives capitalized?

Part B

Directions: Based on your answers to Part A, respond to the statements below.

1. Name a new strength in your writing that you want to continue to use in future assignments.

   _____

2. Name a feature of your writing that you want to improve by reviewing the information in Chapter 3.

   _____

Answers are on page 271.

CHAPTER 4

Description

A descriptive essay tells what something is like. Read the essay topic and descriptive essay below.

--- **TOPIC** ---

Many people dream of their perfect car. What would your perfect car be like?

In your essay, describe your ideal car. Give specific details to show what the car would be like. Use your personal observations, experience, and knowledge.

My dream car is a brand new convertible sports car. I want to have a car like this because it is sleek and speedy, and its engine purrs like a cat. The exterior will be jet black, and it will have special alloy wheels and chrome hubcaps that sparkle brightly in the sun. The interior will have soft brown leather upholstery that feels as smooth as butter, and the rest of the interior will be brown too. I love to listen to music when I drive, so I will get a special stereo sound system with a five-disc CD player. From the mirror, I will hang the red tassel from the graduation cap I wore when I got my GED. The car will have the rich, unmistakable scent of a new car, letting everyone know that this is my first new car.

Answer the following questions:

1. What is topic sentence of this paragraph?

2. What is the writer's dream car like?

3. Give a specific detail that shows readers what the writer's car is like.

4. Would your dream car be like the writer's dream car? Why or why not?

LEARNING TO WRITE: *A Descriptive Essay*

The paragraph on page 000 is an example of descriptive writing. **Descriptive writing** tells readers what a person, place, or thing is like. You can write descriptions about a friend, your family, or a famous star. You can describe your home, downtown, or your workplace. You can write a description of your favorite food, a poster or a painting, or your hobby or collection. Which of the following sentences is an example of descriptive writing?

I bought my car in 2002.

My car is a sturdy sport-utility vehicle.

If you said the second sentence is an example of descriptive writing, you answered correctly. This sentence gives a description of the speaker's car as a sturdy sport-utility vehicle. The first sentence is an example of narration—writing that tells what happened.

EXERCISE 1

Directions: Reread the paragraph on page 47, and answer the questions below.

1. What is the car like? Summarize the description in a few lines.

   _____

   _____

2. What details does the author use to describe the car? List one or two examples.

   _____

   _____

3. Does the paragraph give a strong image of the car? How could the description be stronger? Give an example.

   _____

   _____

Answers are on page 271.

EXERCISE 2

Directions: Read the following essay topics. Which topics require description? Circle the numbers.

1. Everyone has a best friend. Who is your best friend? What is he or she like?

2. Everyone has a memorable event that changes his or her life. What is the most memorable event in your life? Tell what happened. Tell why it changed your life.

3. What is your favorite food? What does it taste like? Look like? Smell like? Why do you like it so much?

4. Some people think that people who drive while talking on cell phones are at a greater risk of causing accidents. For this reason, some people think that talking on a cell phone should be banned while driving. Do you agree? Why or why not?

5. Many people keep pets. Why do people like having pets? Do you have a pet or want to have one? Why or why not?

Answers are on page 271.

A good description gives the reader a vivid, detailed image. For example, which description is better?

That new automobile is really, really fast.

That brand new, bright red sports car is as fast as a jet.

If you said the second sentence is a better description, you are correct. It uses specific adjectives and details to give you a strong image of the car and how fast it can go.

To create strong images, a good writer uses the following tools:

• Specific details

He speedily drove down the tree-lined boulevard. On one side, the lake sparkled. On the other, high-rise apartment houses towered.

• Specific adjectives and adverbs

The body of my car is a **deep crimson.**

The racecar **quickly** circled the oval racetrack and crossed the finish line.

- Comparisons that use the words *as . . . as . . .* and *like*

     I'm **as giddy as** a schoolgirl.

     The engine roars **like a tiger** when you press the accelerator.

- The five senses (sight, smell, touch, taste, sound)

     In the sun my car's hubcaps **sparkle like diamonds.** (*sight*)

     The engine **purrs deeply yet softly.** (*sound*)

Like all good writing, a descriptive paragraph should begin with a topic sentence and contain several supporting sentences.

EXERCISE 3

Directions: Reread the paragraph on page 47 and respond to the following statements.

1. Find the comparisons with *as . . . as . . .* and *like*. Write them on the line.

     _____

2. Find a detail that appeals to the sense of touch. Write it on the line.

     _____

3. Find a detail that appeals to the sense of sight. Write it on the line.

     _____

4. Find a detail that appeals to the sense of smell. Write it on the line.

     _____

5. Think of a detail you might add to the paragraph. Write it on the line. Which sense does it appeal to?

     Detail: _____

     Sense: _____

Answers are on page 271.

EXERCISE 4

Directions: Complete each sentence below by writing appropriate descriptive words in the blanks.

1. The diamond on Lucille's wedding ring was as big as a _____.

2. The sky was a _____, _____ blue.

3. In the dark the cat's eyes glowed like _____.

4. The waves hit the beach _____.

5. The car drove _____ and _____ up the mountain road.

Answers are on page 271.

EXERCISE 5

Directions: Rewrite each sentence below so it is a stronger description.

Example: The room smelled bad.

The room stank like rotten Limburger cheese.

1. The house was old.

   _____

2. I want to buy a speedy car.

   _____

3. That man is very handsome.

   _____

4. Would you like fries with that?

   _____

Answers are on page 271.

EXPANDING IDEAS: *Idea Maps*

An **idea map** is a graphic organizer that can help you gather ideas for a descriptive essay. It is similar to an idea circle but gives more details. An idea map shows you the relationship among ideas by using circles and lines. Look at the idea map created by the writer of the paragraph on an ideal car.

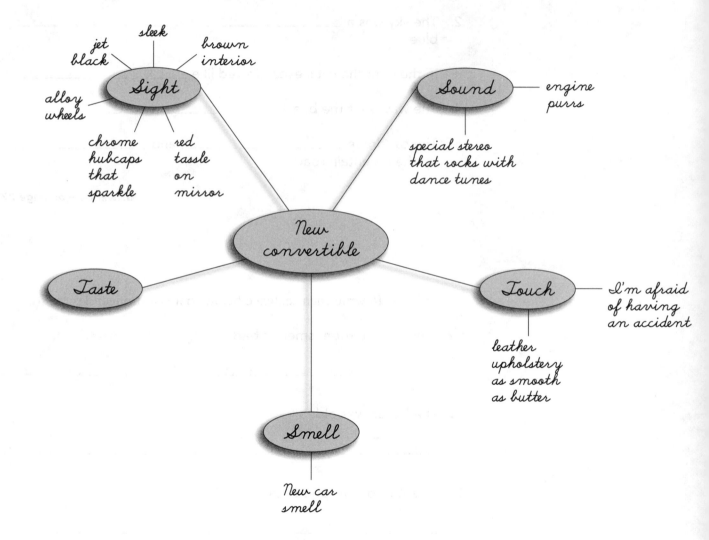

The writer put the main idea in the center of the idea map. Then, the five senses were used to gather ideas for the essay. Of course, the sense of taste was not relevant to an essay on a car, so no ideas were included that related to taste. Notice that the writer did not put all the details in the idea chart. More details were added while the essay was being written.

EXERCISE 6

Directions: Think of a main idea for the following GED essay topic.
Write it on the line below and complete the blank idea map.

─────── **T O P I C** ───────

Everyone has a favorite place. What is yours?

In your essay, describe your favorite place. Give specific details to show what the place is like. Use your personal observations, experience and knowledge.

Main idea: _____

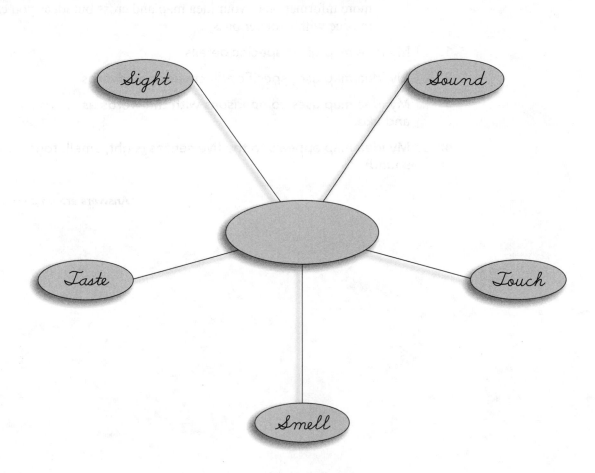

Answers are on page 271.

After you complete your idea map, you should check it. You should make sure that all the ideas are relevant to the topic. You should also make sure that you have enough ideas.

Look again at the idea map on page 52. Which idea is not relevant? Cross it off. What idea would you add? Put it on the idea map.

If you said that you would cross off the idea *I am afraid of having an accident*, you are correct. This idea does not help describe the car. Possible ideas you could add to the idea map include information on the car's shiny finish, special power locks, or mechanical convertible top.

EXERCISE 7

Directions: Review the idea map you created in Exercise 6. Be sure that your ideas are specific and relevant. Use the following checklist. Add more information to your idea map and cross out ideas you can replace with stronger ones.

1. ☐ My idea map gives specific details.

2. ☐ My idea map uses specific adjectives and adverbs.

3. ☐ My idea map uses comparisons with the words *as . . . as . . .* and *like.*

4. ☐ My idea map appeals to the five senses (sight, smell, touch, taste, sound).

Answers are on page 271.

EXERCISE 8

Part A

Directions: Read the following GED essay topic. Complete the idea map below.

──────────── **T O P I C** ────────────

What is your favorite room in your house?

In your essay, describe your favorite room. Explain why you like it. Use your personal observations, experience, and knowledge.

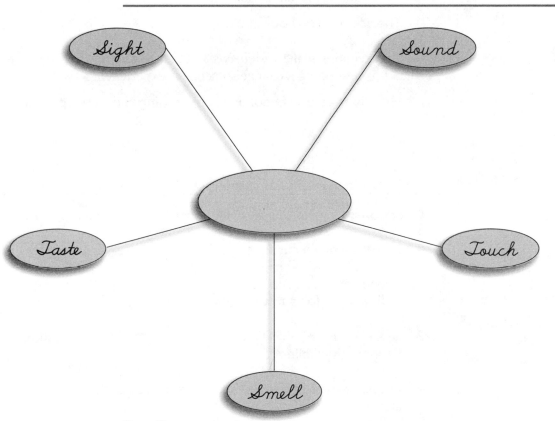

Part B

Directions: Review your idea map. Use the following checklist.

1. ☐ My idea map gives specific details.

2. ☐ My idea map uses specific adjectives and adverbs.

3. ☐ My idea map uses comparisons with the words *as . . . as . . .* and *like.*

4. ☐ My idea map appeals to the five senses (sight, smell, touch, taste, and sound).

Answers are on page 271.

LOOKING AT LANGUAGE: *Description and Details*

Linking Verbs

Linking verbs are used to link the subject with a word that tells more about it—usually an adjective and/or another noun. Common linking verbs are *be (is, are), seem, sound, look, feel, taste, smell,* and *become.*

A Mustang **is** a sleek car.

That car **looks** speedy.

Linking verbs are usually used in the simple present, past, and future tenses and in the present perfect tense.

The soup **tasted** delicious.

An exception is the verb *become.* It can be used in the progressive tense when it is describing a change someone is experiencing.

He is in medical school. He **is becoming** a cancer specialist.

EXERCISE 9

Directions: Complete each sentence below with an appropriate linking verb.

1. I want to buy a car that _____ very fast.

2. These towels _____ damp. Please put them back in the dryer for a few minutes.

3. After he got his GED he _____ a student at Bright Community College.

4. I'm not sure if I believe him. His story _____ strange.

5. Look at you! You _____ a beautiful woman right before my eyes.

Answers are on page 271.

Adjectives and Adverbs

An **adjective** gives more information about a noun or pronoun. An **adverb** gives more information about a verb or adjective.

He has a **slow** car. *(adjective)*

He **slowly** drove home. *(adverb)*

He is **very** busy today. *(adverb)*

Some adjectives and adverbs have the same form.

She always drives **fast.** *(adverb)*

She's a **fast** driver. *(adjective)*

EXERCISE 10

Directions: Complete each sentence below with an appropriate adjective or adverb.

1. He served his guests some _____ pie for dessert.

2. Could you _____ go to the supermarket and get some milk for dinner? It's almost dinnertime.

3. That's a _____ wonderful idea!

4. My boss and I get along _____.

5. Mrs. Taylor's car is a really ugly color: _____.

6. I can hardly understand you. Please talk _____.

7. I didn't get much sleep during my vacation. The bed in my hotel was very _____.

8. Drive _____ on your trip to Tennessee.

9. I don't like this cake. It tastes _____.

10. Mr. Applebee drives _____.

Answers are on page 271.

Other Details

In addition to adjectives and adverbs, there are several ways to give more detail.

- Use *as...as* and *like*.

    This strawberry-rhubarb pie smells **as good as** it looks!

    These cookies taste **like homemade.**

- Use prepositional phrases. A **prepositional phrase** consists of a preposition and a noun. Prepositional phrases often give information about a noun or a verb. Common prepositions include *with, on, in, at, under, over, without,* and *through.*

    I want a car **with power steering and antilock brakes.**

    Her car had a flat tire **on route 66.**

- Use dependent clauses. A **dependent clause** has a subject and a verb. It is joined to the rest of a sentence with a subordinating conjunction such as *that, when,* or *where.* A dependent clause usually gives more information about another word in the sentence.

    I want that car **if it can go from zero to sixty in ten seconds.**
    (The clause gives more information about why the writer will buy the car.)

    I bought a new car **when my old one broke down.**
    (The clause gives more information about when the writer bought the car.)

EXERCISE 11

Directions: Rewrite the following sentences with more detail. Use adjectives, adverbs, prepositional phrases, and clauses.

1. Their vacation was fun. _____

2. Ms. Espinoza is very nice. _____

3. That house is old. _____

4. That dog is fat. _____

5. The soup tasted bad. _____

Answers are on page 271.

GED Connection

Directions: Choose the <u>one best answer</u> to each question.

My Street

(1) I live on Green Street, a quiet side street about two miles from downtown. (2) All of the neighbors are friendly and politely. (3) There are two bus stops nearby, and a market with wonderful fruits and vegetables is in walking distance. (4) At night there's not a lot of traffic. (5) In fact it's as quiet as can be. (6) Everyone takes great care of their yards. (7) In spring the red, yellow, and purple flowers are looking great in people's flower beds.

1. **Sentence 2: All of the neighbors are <u>friendly and politely</u>.**

   What is the best way to write the underlined portion of the text? If the original is the best way, choose option (1).

   (1) friendly and politely
   (2) friendly and polite
   (3) friend and polite
   (4) friendly, polite
   (5) friendly, politely

2. **Sentence 3: There are two bus stops nearby, and a market with wonderful fruits and vegetables is in walking distance.**

   What correction should be made to sentence 3?

   (1) change *There are* to *There is*
   (2) change *bus stops* to *bus stop*
   (3) remove the comma after *nearby*
   (4) change *vegetables is* to *vegetables are*
   (5) no correction is necessary

3. **Sentence 7: In spring the red, yellow, and purple flowers are looking great in people's flower beds.**

   What correction should be made to sentence 7?

   (1) change *are looking great* to *look great*
   (2) change *are looking great* to *are looking greatly*
   (3) insert a comma after *great*
   (4) replace *are* with *is*
   (5) no correction is necessary

Answers are on page 272.

WRITING A GED ESSAY: *Description*

- Good descriptive writing uses specific language, comparisons with *as ...as* and *like*, and appeals to the five senses.

- An idea map is a good way to gather ideas for a descriptive essay.

- In descriptive writing special attention should be given to the use of linking verbs, adjectives and adverbs, and comparisons using *like* and *as...as*. Phrases and clauses should be used to give details.

GED Practice

Directions: Use the four steps of the writing process to create a one-paragraph descriptive essay that responds to the following GED essay topic. Follow the steps below.

--- T O P I C ---

Many people dream of their perfect car. What would your perfect car be like?

In your essay, describe your ideal car. Give specific details to show what the car would be like. Use your personal observations, experience, and knowledge.

---

1. **Gather Ideas**

   Read the essay topic and think of the main idea for your one-paragraph essay. Write your main idea in the center of the idea map. Then fill in the map.

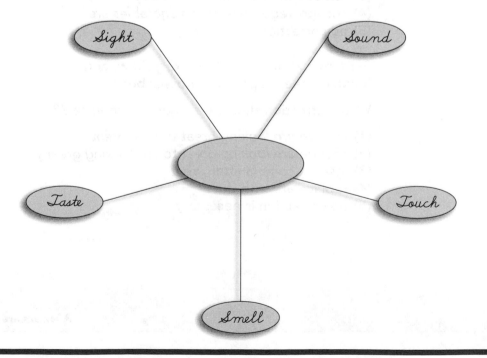

2. **Organize Your Ideas**

   A. Review your idea map. Be sure your ideas are specific and relevant. Use the following checklist. Add more information to your idea map and cross off ideas you can replace with stronger ideas.

   1. ☐ My idea map gives specific details.

   2. ☐ My idea map uses specific adjectives and adverbs.

   3. ☐ My idea map uses comparisons with the words *as . . . as . . .* and *like.*

   4. ☐ My idea map appeals to the five senses (sight, smell, touch, taste, and sound).

   B. Decide the order you will use to write your essay. Number the ideas in this order. Cross off any ideas that are not relevant.

3. **Write Your Essay**

   Use your organized idea map to write a good one-paragraph essay. Do not spend a lot of time worrying about grammar, punctuation, or spelling. You will check for mistakes after you write your essay.

   _____

   _____

   _____

   _____

   _____

   _____

   _____

   _____

   _____

   _____

   _____

   _____

   _____

   _____

_____

_____

_____

_____

_____

_____

_____

_____

_____

_____

_____

_____

_____

4. Revise Your Essay

    A. Check your essay's ideas using the following list.

        1. ☐ My essay gives specific details.

        2. ☐ My essay uses specific adjectives and adverbs.

        3. ☐ My essay uses comparisons with the words _as . . . as . . ._ and _like._

        4. ☐ My essay appeals to the five senses (sight, smell, touch, taste, and sound).

    B. Check your essay for standards of Edited American English.

        1. ☐ My essay uses capitalization correctly.

        2. ☐ The words are spelled correctly.

        3. ☐ Linking verbs are in the future, simple present, present perfect, or simple past tenses.

        4. ☐ Adjectives and adverbs are used correctly.

Answers are on page 272.

Writing and Life

Directions: Use the four steps of the writing process to create a one-paragraph descriptive essay that responds to the following essay topic.

———— T O P I C ————

What does it take to be a good parent?

In your essay, describe the characteristics of a good parent. Give specific details to explain your views. Use your personal observations, experience, and knowledge.

_____

_____

_____

_____

_____

_____

_____

_____

_____

_____

_____

_____

_____

_____

_____

Answers are on page 272.

Self-Assessment

Part A

Directions: Ask your instructor or a friend to review your work on page 63, or review it yourself. Answer the following questions. Write **yes** or **no** on the appropriate lines below.

1. _____ Is the first line of the essay indented?

2. _____ Does the essay have a clear topic sentence and several supporting sentences?

3 _____ Do the supporting sentences back up the topic sentence?

4. _____ Do the supporting sentences include details, specific adjectives and adverbs, and comparisons with the words *like* and *as . . . as . . .* ?

5. _____ Do the ideas appeal to the five senses?

6. _____ Does the essay contain descriptive language?

Part B

Directions: Based on your answers to Part A, respond to the statements below.

1. Name a new strength in your writing that you want to continue to use in future assignments.

_____

2. Name a feature of your writing that you want to improve by reviewing the information in Chapter 4.

_____

Answers are on page 272.

CHAPTER 5

Process

A process essay tells how to do something. It lists the steps and the order in which to perform them. Read the essay topic and process essay below.

───────────────── **TOPIC** ─────────────────

What is your favorite late-night snack?

Write an essay explaining how to prepare your favorite late-night snack.

───

    For a midnight snack, nothing beats a peanut butter and jelly sandwich. To make a PB & J, I get out two slices of whole wheat bread. Then I spread a thick layer of low-fat peanut butter on one slice of bread. You can use crunchy or smooth peanut butter. I like to use low-fat peanut butter for my sandwiches. Then I add a thin layer of grape jelly on top of the peanut butter. Finally, I add the top slice of bread, put the sandwich on a plate, and cut the sandwich into halves. Then I have the perfect snack to eat while watching the late news. Try a PB & J yourself! It's a delicious snack that's easy to make.

Answer the following questions:

1. What is the topic sentence of the paragraph?

2. What is a PB & J?

3. What food do you need to make a PB & J?

4. What's the first step in making a PB & J?

5. What's the last step in making a PB & J?

6. Do you think a PB & J is a good late-night snack? Why or why not?

LEARNING TO WRITE: *A Process Essay*

The paragraph on page 65 is an example of process writing. **Process writing** tells the reader how to do something. It tells you the steps and the order in which to perform them. A process essay can tell how to change a diaper, repair a car, or cook a meal. A process essay can tell how to use a computer, a blender, or an electric drill. A process essay can give instructions on how to start a car or how to drive to a certain place. Look at the following groups of sentences. Which group lists the steps in a process?

1. Our little fishing boat was securely tied to the pier. It bobbed slightly in the sparkling, crystal-clear water as the waves lapped up and down. The little outboard motor sat idle waiting for us to start it.

2. To get to the best fishing spot in Lake Harrison, start your motor and go due east for four miles until you come to Cabot's Cove. Then look for the little inlet just north of Cabot's Cove. Quietly row to the inlet without disturbing the fish.

If you said the second group of sentences describes a process, you are correct. They explain how to get to a certain place in Lake Harrison. The first group of sentences is a description of the fishing boat.

EXERCISE 1

Directions: Reread the paragraph on page 65 and answer the questions below.

1. What items do you need to make a PB & J?

   _____

2. How many steps are needed to make a PB & J?

   _____

3. Is a PB & J easy or hard to make?

   _____

4. Does the paragraph give complete directions on how to make a PB & J? Or is information missing? What information? Why do you think so?

   _____

Answers are on page 272.

When you read an essay topic, some key words and phrases such as *how, steps,* and *what do you do to...* will tell you if you need to explain a process in your essay. Read the following essay topics. Which one is for a process essay?

How do you make a chicken taco salad?

Who was the most influential person in your life? Why?

If you said the first essay topic is for a process essay, you are correct. It asks you to write an essay explaining the steps, or process, for making a certain kind of food. The second topic asks you to describe an influential person.

EXERCISE 2

Part A

Directions: Read the following essay topics. Which topics are about a process? Which are about a description? Write **P** for process or **D** for description on the appropriate lines.

1. _____ How do you frost a birthday cake?

2. _____ What does poison ivy look like?

3. _____ Name the steps for putting gas in a car.

4. _____ Who is the most attractive movie star in your opinion? Why?

5. _____ How do you give a dog a bath?

Part B

Directions: Look again at the essay topics in Part A. Which words helped you decide which topics were for a process essay? Circle the words.

Answers are on page 272.

Figuring Out What You Need

In order to describe a process, you must know all of the things you are going to need to complete the process. Look at the following list of items that the writer created for making a peanut butter and jelly sandwich. The writer forgot one item. Can you figure out the missing item? Write it on the line below.

two slices of bread

peanut butter

grape jelly

a knife

a toaster

_____

What did you add to the list? If you added a plate, your answer is correct. The instructions clearly say to put the sandwich on a plate before cutting it in half.

EXERCISE 3

Part A

Directions: Read each process topic below. Make a list of the items you will need to complete the process.

1. Washing a dog

   _____

   _____

   _____

2. Starting a car

   _____

   _____

   _____

3. Getting ready for work

    _____

    _____

    _____

4. Heating a can of soup

    _____

    _____

    _____

    _____

Part B

Directions: Think of a process that you often do and write it below. What items do you need to carry out the process? Write the items on the lines below.

Process: _____

What you need:

_____   _____   _____

_____   _____   _____

_____   _____   _____

Answers are on page 272.

Ordering the Steps

To write a good process essay, the steps need to be in the correct order. Look at the following paragraph. Circle the step that is out of order.

> To barbecue chicken, take a whole, fresh chicken and cut it into parts the night before. Put the chicken in a bowl. Then start a charcoal fire outdoors. Spray lighter fluid on the charcoal and light the charcoal. After the coals are hot and glowing red, put the chicken on the fire. Cover the cut-up chicken with barbecue sauce and let it sit overnight in the fridge. Turn the chicken frequently until it's done. Serve on a new serving platter or in a bowl, not on the same dish you used for the raw chicken.

If you circled *Cover the cut-up chicken with barbecue sauce and let it sit overnight in the fridge*, you are correct. This is the second step. It comes after cutting up the chicken into parts.

EXERCISE 4

Directions: Look at the steps for making a peanut butter and jelly sandwich. Put them in order. Write numbers from 1 (first) to 6 (last).

a. _____ Add the top slice of bread.

b. _____ Get out two slices of whole wheat bread.

c. _____ Add a thin layer of grape jelly on top of the peanut butter.

d. _____ Cut the sandwich into halves.

e. _____ Put the sandwich on a plate.

f. _____ Spread low-fat peanut butter on one slice of bread.

Answers are on page 272.

EXPANDING IDEAS: *Flow Charts*

A **flow chart** is a graphic organizer that can help you gather and organize ideas for a process essay. In a flow chart, you put the steps in order from first to last. Look at the flow chart created by the writer of the paragraph about peanut butter and jelly sandwiches.

Get out two slices of bread.	Spread peanut butter on one slice.
Add grape jelly on top of peanut butter.	Add the top slice of bread.
Put the sandwich on a plate.	Cut sandwich into halves.

As you can see, the writer used the flow chart to figure out everything needed to make the sandwich as well as to put the steps in order.

EXERCISE 5

Directions: Read the following GED essay topic. Then complete the flow chart below.

——————— T O P I C ———————

How do you do your laundry?

Write an essay explaining how you wash your clothes each week.

Items needed: _____

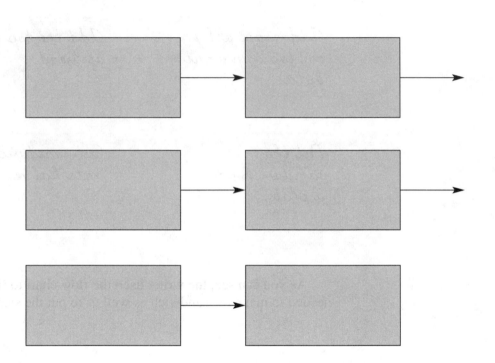

Answers are on page 272.

Checking Your Flow Chart

After you complete your flow chart, you should check it. You should be sure that you have listed all of the things you need and all the right steps. You should be sure that the steps are in the right order.

Look at the following flow chart for washing a car. Two things are wrong with this flow chart: An item is missing, and a step is in the wrong order. Add the missing item to the list. Circle the step that is in the wrong order.

Items needed: car, hose, bucket, rags

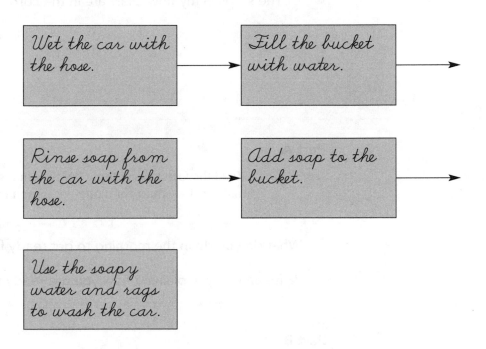

If you said that soap is missing from the list of items, you are correct. The step that is in the wrong order is *Rinse the soap from the car with the hose.* This step should come after washing the car with the soapy water.

EXERCISE 6

Directions: Review the flow chart you created in Exercise 5. Be sure that you have listed all of the items you need, included all the required steps, and eliminated any extra steps. Use the following checklist.

1. ☐ My flow chart lists all the items I need.

2. ☐ My flow chart includes all the necessary steps.

3. ☐ My flow chart has no extra steps.

4. ☐ The steps in my flow chart are in the correct order.

Answers are on page 272.

EXERCISE 7

Part A

Directions: Read the GED essay topic below. On a separate sheet of paper, make a flow chart for a one-paragraph essay.

——————————————— T O P I C ———————————————

What do you do in the morning to get ready for work or school?

Write an essay explaining how you get ready for work or school.

Part B

Directions: Review your flow chart. Use the following checklist.

1. ☐ My flow chart lists all the items I need.

2. ☐ My flow chart includes all the necessary steps.

3. ☐ My flow chart has no extra steps.

4. ☐ The steps in my flow chart are in the correct order.

LOOKING AT LANGUAGE: *Transitions and Tense*

Sequence Words

A good process essay will use **sequence words** to help the reader understand the order of the steps. These words include ordinal numbers (*first, second, third, fourth*) and adverbs of sequence (*next, then, finally*, and *last*). When these words come at the beginning of a sentence, they are followed by a comma. Look at the following paragraph:

> You should **first** get out four hamburger buns. **Second,** spread mustard on the top of each bun. **Third,** put a slice of turkey and a slice of Swiss cheese in each bun. **Then,** wrap each bun in a sheet of aluminum foil. **Next,** put the sandwiches on a baking sheet and put them in a 350-degree oven for 20 minutes. **Finally,** remove the sandwiches from the oven and serve them piping hot.

EXERCISE 8

Part A

Directions: Rewrite the paragraph below using sequence words.

> To change the batteries in a smoke detector, get a stepladder and a new battery. Put the stepladder under the smoke detector and climb up. Take the cover off the smoke detector. Take out the old battery. Put in the new battery. Put the cover back on the smoke detector. Press the test button to make sure the smoke detector is working. If the detector rings, the alarm is fine. Climb down the stepladder and put it away. Throw away the used battery.

_____

_____

_____

_____

_____

_____

Part B

Directions: You want someone to change the batteries in a flashlight. Write instructions using sequence words.

_____

_____

_____

_____

Answers are on page 272.

Simple Present Tense

One common way to write a process essay is with the **simple present tense**.

> First, you **put** seventy-five cents in the soda machine. Then you **press** the button for the kind of soda you want. Your soda **comes** out at the bottom of the machine.

The simple present tense is also used to show habitual or regular actions.

> I always get up at 5:00 A.M.

The simple present tense is formed by using the base form of the verb (the verb without any ending), such as *put* and *press,* or by adding a final *s* or *es,* such as *puts* or *presses.* In general, verbs that end in a "hissing" sound *(s, sh, ch, x,* and *z)* take the *es* ending. Look at the following chart:

Subject	Verb
I, you, we, they	put, press
he, she, it	puts, presses

EXERCISE 9

Directions: For each sentence below, write the verb in parentheses in the simple present tense.

1. Amanda _____ (work) at Standard Hospital Supply Company.

2. She always _____ (arrive) at work at 8:00 A.M.

3. She _____ (clock) in and

   _____ (go) to her workstation.

4. She works with Martha Lee. They _____ (pack) customer orders in the warehouse.

5. Martha and Amanda _____ (have) to work quickly and carefully.

6. They _____ (need) to make sure that customers get the correct supplies.

7. Sometimes a customer _____ (get) the wrong supplies.

8. Then the customer _____ (call) the customer

   service department and _____ (complain).

9. When that _____ (happen), Martha and Amanda

   _____ (send) a replacement order to the customer.

10. In the end, the customer _____ (receive) the correct supplies.

Answers are on page 273.

Imperatives

An **imperative** is a command. Imperatives are another way to write a process essay. An imperative is formed by using the base form of the verb without a subject. The subject of an imperative is always understood to be *you*.

Put a quarter in the gum machine. Then **turn** the handle.

EXERCISE 10

Part A

Directions: Rewrite each sentence below as an imperative.

1. To make a root beer float, you put two scoops of ice cream in a tall glass.

   _____

2. Then, you pour cold root beer over the ice cream.

   _____

3. Next, you top the ice cream with some whipped cream.

   _____

4. Last, you put a cherry on top of the float.

   _____

Part B

Directions: Write a paragraph in which you explain how to make an ice cream sundae. Use imperatives.

   _____

   _____

   _____

   _____

   _____

   _____

   _____

   _____

Answers are on page 273.

GED Connection

Directions: Choose the <u>one best answer</u> to each question.

Nationwide Office Supplies

Instructions for Packing Customer Orders

(1) In order for our Internet customers to receive the best possible customer service, it is important that all employees follow these simple instructions. (2) When you get an order ticket from the printer, first read it carefully. (3) Then, go to the shelves in the warehouse and get the items that the customer want. (4) Put all of the items in a shipping box. (5) Then seal the box. (6) Count the total number of items as you put them in the box. (7) Make sure that the number of items in the box agrees with the total number of items printed on the bottom of the order ticket. (8) Last, place the shipping label on the outside of the box and take the box to the mailroom.

1. **Sentence 2: When you get an order ticket from the printer, first read it carefully.**

   What correction should be made to sentence 2?

   (1) add a comma after *order*
   (2) remove the comma after *printer*
   (3) add a comma after *first*
   (4) add a comma after *it*
   (5) no correction is necessary

2. **Sentence 3: Then, go to the shelves in the warehouse and get the items that the customer want.**

   What correction should be made to sentence 3?

   (1) remove the comma after *Then*
   (2) change *go* to *goes*
   (3) add a comma after *and*
   (4) change *want* to *wants*
   (5) no correction is necessary

3. **Sentence 5: Then seal the box.**

   Which revision would make the paragraph more effective?

   (1) move sentence 5 to follow sentence 3
   (2) move sentence 5 to follow sentence 6
   (3) move sentence 5 to follow sentence 7
   (4) remove sentence 5
   (5) no revision is necessary

Answers are on page **273.**

WRITING A GED ESSAY: *Process*

- Process writing tells the steps you follow to make or do something.

- Good process writing includes all of the items needed, the steps that must be followed, and the order in which the steps must be given.

- A flow chart is a good graphic organizer to use to gather and organize ideas for a process essay.

- A good process essay uses sequence words (such as *first*, *then*, *last*, and *finally*) to indicate the sequence of the steps.

- A good process essay can use the simple present tense or imperatives to show the actions.

GED Practice

Directions: Use the four steps of the writing process to create a one-paragraph process essay that responds to the following GED essay topic. Follow the steps below.

--- **T O P I C** ---

What is your favorite late-night snack?

Write an essay explaining how to prepare your favorite late-night snack.

1. **Gather Ideas**

   Read the essay topic and think of the main idea for your one-paragraph essay. Write your main idea on the line below, and complete the flow chart.

   Main idea: _____

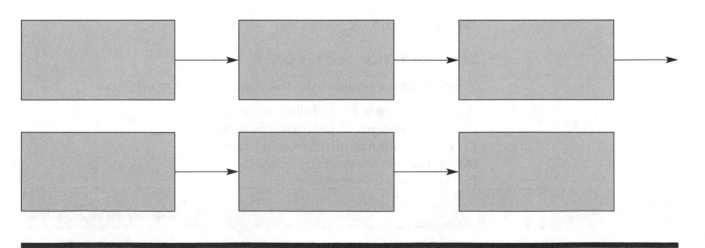

2. Organize Your Ideas

Review your flow chart. Use the following checklist. Add missing information and cross off extra information.

1. ☐ My flow chart lists all the items I need.

2. ☐ My flow chart includes all the necessary steps.

3. ☐ My flow chart has no extra steps.

4. ☐ The steps in my flow chart are in the correct order.

3. Write Your Essay

Use your flow chart to write a good one-paragraph essay. Do not spend a lot of time worrying about grammar, punctuation, or spelling. You will check for mistakes after you write your essay.

_____

_____

_____

_____

_____

_____

_____

_____

_____

_____

_____

_____

_____

_____

_____

_____

_____

_____

_____

_____

_____

_____

_____

_____

_____

4. Revise Your Essay

   A. Check your essay's ideas using the following list.

      1. ☐ My essay lists all the items I need.

      2. ☐ My essay includes all the necessary steps.

      3. ☐ My essay has no extra steps.

      4. ☐ The steps in my essay are in the correct order.

   B. Check your essay for standards of Edited American English.

      1. ☐ My essay uses sequence words.

      2. ☐ Sequence words at the beginning of sentences are followed by a comma.

      3. ☐ My essay uses the simple present tense or imperatives to show the actions.

      4. ☐ Verbs agree with their subjects.

Answers are on page 273.

Writing and Life

Directions: Use the four steps of the writing process to create a one-paragraph process essay that responds to the following essay topic.

──────────── **T O P I C** ────────────

How do you study for an important test such as the GED?

In your essay, explain how to study for a test like the GED. Use your personal observations, experience, and knowledge.

──────────────────────────────────

_____

_____

_____

_____

_____

_____

_____

_____

_____

_____

_____

_____

_____

Answers are on page 273.

Self-Assessment

Part A

Directions: Ask your instructor or a friend to review your work on page 83, or review it yourself. Answer the following questions. Write **yes** or **no** on the appropriate lines below.

1. _____ Does the essay list all the necessary items?

2. _____ Does the essay include all the necessary steps?

3. _____ Does the essay have any extra steps?

4. _____ Are the steps in the essay in the correct order?

5. _____ Does the essay use sequence words? Are the sequence words at the beginning of sentences followed by a comma?

6. _____ Does the essay use the simple present tense or imperatives to show the actions?

7. _____ Do the verbs in the essay agree with their subjects?

Part B

Directions: Based on your answers to Part A, respond to the statements below.

1. Name a new strength in your writing that you want to continue to use in future assignments.

   _____

2. Name a feature of your writing that you want to improve by reviewing the information in Chapter 5.

   _____

Answers are on page 273.

CHAPTER 6

The Three-Paragraph Essay

A three-paragraph essay is longer and more complex than a one-paragraph essay. A three-paragraph essay is useful when you need more than one paragraph to explain your ideas. Read the following essay topic and three-paragraph essay.

TOPIC

What is your favorite sport or pastime? Why do you like it?

In your essay, state your favorite sport or pastime. Give specific reasons about why you like it. Use your personal observations, experience, and knowledge.

85

There are plenty of great sports, and I love them all. Some sports, such as golf, are fun to watch. Others, like baseball and basketball, are fun to watch and to play. However, if I had to identify one sport as my very favorite, I would have to say that it is NASCAR racing. I love watching NASCAR racing because it is an exciting sport that requires driving skill and mechanical ability.

For me, NASCAR racing is an exciting sport that requires the ability to handle and tune a car. I love hearing the roar of powerful motors as the cars race around the track. It's really gripping when a car tries to pass another car and break into the lead. However, winning involves more than just driving fast—a driver has to be able to handle the car well. A driver needs to take turns at the right speed so that the car does not spin out or hit another car. Drivers also have to be able to pass one another without colliding. One mark of a great driver is the ability to break out of the pack and suddenly take the lead. Finally, drivers need to be able to keep their cars in top condition. A good driver is the leader of a team of mechanics who knows how to keep a car's engine in top form so that it can perform at its peak.

To conclude, I love NASCAR racing because of the combination of skill and excitement. I hope that someday I can attend a major NASCAR race in person so that I can see the cars, meet the mechanics and drivers, and see firsthand how the drivers handle their cars on the track. Until then, I am going to continue to watch NASCAR races on TV every chance I get!

Answer the following questions.

1. What is the writer's favorite sport?

2. Why does the writer like it so much?

3. Does the writer give plenty of reasons to back up the main idea?

4. What is your favorite sport or pastime?

LEARNING TO WRITE: *A Three-Paragraph Essay*

As you saw in Chapter 3, an essay can be one or more paragraphs long. You have already had experience writing one-paragraph essays, and now you are ready to move on to a longer, more-complex kind of essay, the three-paragraph essay.

As you know, a one-paragraph essay has a very specific structure:

1. A topic sentence that introduces the main idea

2. A number of supporting sentences that back up the topic sentence

3. A concluding sentence that sums up the main idea of the paragraph and brings the paragraph to a close

A **three-paragraph essay** has a similar structure:

1. An introductory paragraph that gives a general sense of the main idea

2. A body paragraph that contains a number of specific supporting sentences that back up the main idea

3. A concluding paragraph that sums up the main idea and brings the essay to a close

A three-paragraph essay has room for more information and detail than a one-paragraph essay. A three-paragraph essay allows more opportunities for presenting the topic in the introductory paragraph and for relating it to broader ideas in the concluding paragraph.

EXERCISE 1

Directions: Label each paragraph in the essay on page 86 with the appropriate term below.

Introductory paragraph

Body paragraph

Concluding paragraph

Answers are on page 273.

Introductory Paragraph

The job of the **introductory paragraph** is to build the reader's interest and to state the main idea of the essay. Usually an introductory paragraph is organized from general to more specific. The last sentence in the introductory paragraph is called the **thesis statement**. It gives the main idea of the essay and also indicates the type of information that will be contained in the body paragraph. Look again at the essay on page 86. Circle the thesis statement.

If you circled *I love watching NASCAR racing because it is an exciting sport that requires driving skill and mechanical ability*, you are correct. This sentence is last in the paragraph and gives a specific overview of what will follow in the body paragraph.

EXERCISE 2

Part A

Directions: Look at the thesis statement for the essay on page 86. What kind of information does it say will be in the essay on NASCAR racing? Write words or phrases on the lines below.

1. _____

2. _____

3. _____

Part B

Directions: Now look at the body paragraph on page 86. Does it contain the information you wrote on the lines?

Part C

Directions: Based on your answers to Parts A and B, do you think the thesis statement is a good one? Why? Write a few words on the lines below.

_____

_____

Answers are on page 273.

Body Paragraph

The job of the **body paragraph** is to state the main idea of the essay in detail. Each of the sentences in the body paragraph must back up or explain the ideas in the thesis statement. Usually sentences in the body paragraph are very specific. A good body paragraph also begins with a topic sentence. Look at the body paragraph on page 86. Circle the topic sentence.

If you circled *For me, NASCAR racing is an exciting sport that requires the ability to handle and tune a car,* you are correct. Now compare the thesis statement with the topic sentence. Which is more specific?

Thesis statement (introductory paragraph):
I love watching NASCAR racing because it is an exciting sport that requires driving skill and mechanical ability.

Topic sentence (body paragraph):
For me, NASCAR racing is an exciting sport that requires the ability to handle and tune a car.

The topic sentence is more specific than the thesis statement. In a good three-paragraph essay, the topic sentence of the body paragraph restates the thesis statement in more-specific words.

Now look at the rest of the sentences in the paragraph. Notice how they are all very specific and give facts to back up the topic sentence. For example, the sentence *Drivers need to take turns at the right speed so that the car does not spin out or hit another car* specifically backs up *the ability to handle and tune a car* in the topic sentence.

EXERCISE 3

Directions: Which idea does each body sentence back up? Write the appropriate letter on each line below.

a. NASCAR racing is an exciting sport.

b. NASCAR racing requires driving skill and the ability to handle a car.

c. NASCAR racing requires skills to tune a car.

1. _____ It's really gripping when a car tries to pass another driver and break into the lead.

2. _____ A good driver is the leader of a team of mechanics who knows how to keep a car's engine in top form so that it can perform at its peak.

3. _____ One mark of a great driver is the ability to break out of the pack and suddenly take the lead.

Answers are on page 273.

EXERCISE 4

Directions: Read each pair of sentences below. Decide which one is general and which one is specific. Write **G** for general or **S** for specific on the appropriate line.

1. _____ I love crafts.

   _____ Last month I finished knitting a sweater for my daughter's new baby.

2. _____ I think that of all my free-time activities, running in the park is my favorite.

   _____ Getting exercise is a favorite pastime of many people.

3. _____ It's a good idea for children to learn to play musical instruments.

   _____ Juanito has played the cello for six years.

4. _____ Ms. Collier loves to cook in her free time.

   _____ She makes delicious grape jelly in August.

5. _____ I love to watch soap operas on TV.

   _____ *All My Children* is my favorite.

Answers are on page 273.

Concluding Paragraph

The **concluding paragraph** should bring the three-paragraph essay to a smooth ending by summing up the main ideas of the essay and then relating them to broader issues. Usually a good concluding paragraph is organized from specific to general. The first sentence of the concluding paragraph should restate or sum up the thesis statement. Look at the first sentence of the concluding paragraph of the essay on page 86. Notice how it sums up the main idea of the essay (*NASCAR racing is a good sport because it is exciting and requires skill.*):

> To conclude, I love NASCAR racing because of the combination of skill and excitement.

Reread the concluding paragraph. How does the writer broaden ideas and relate them to other, larger ideas? The writer restates his interest in his favorite sport by relating it to broader issues—his dream of one day viewing a NASCAR event in person and his present interest in watching NASCAR races on TV.

EXERCISE 5

Part A

Directions: Read the paragraphs of the three-paragraph essay below. Number them in the correct order. Write **1** for the introductory paragraph, **2** for the body paragraph, and **3** for the concluding paragraph.

(A) _____

Good blues songs express strong feelings about love and life. Blues songs are about the pain of a lost love or family member who has passed away. The words and the music combine to vividly express the feelings and emotions that all of us experience in life whether we are rich or poor, young or old.

(B) _____

One thing I love to do is listen to music. I like all kinds of music. I love dance music, jazz, blues, and even some classical music. However, one kind of music is my very favorite: blues. Listening to blues is my favorite pastime because this music is so expressive and emotional.

(C) _____

For these reasons, the blues is my favorite form of music, and I listen to it every chance I get. I hope that younger blues artists will continue to emerge so that this art form can continue to grow and flourish.

Part B

Directions: Look again at the three-paragraph essay. Underline the thesis statement and circle the topic sentence of the body paragraph.

Answers are on page 273.

EXPANDING IDEAS: *Essay Diagrams*

A good way to visualize the structure of a three-paragraph essay is with an **essay diagram**.

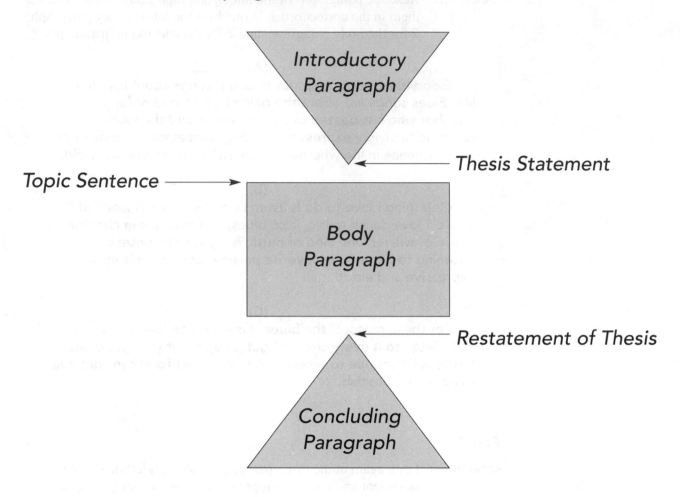

An essay diagram shows the nature of each paragraph in a three-paragraph essay.

- The introductory paragraph begins with a general statement and builds towards a more specific thesis statement.

- The body paragraph begins with a topic sentence, which gives an idea of how the paragraph will be organized. Usually, the topic sentence is a restatement of the thesis statement.

- The concluding paragraph is organized from specific to general. The first sentence of the concluding paragraph summarizes the main ideas of the body paragraph, and the rest of the sentences relate these ideas to broader and more general topics.

EXERCISE 6

Directions: Match each type of sentence in the first column with the paragraph it belongs to in the second column. Use the essay diagram on page 92 to help you.

1. _____ Sentences with specific detail

2. _____ Thesis statement

3. _____ Sentences relating the ideas to larger ideas

4. _____ Sentences summing up the main ideas of the body

5. _____ Topic sentence

a. introductory paragraph

b. body paragraph

c. concluding paragraph

Answers are on page 273.

An essay diagram is useful after you have gathered and organized your ideas and are ready to start writing your essay. You can use an essay diagram to remind you of the structure of a three-paragraph essay. It can help you remember to include an introductory paragraph with a thesis statement, a body paragraph with a topic sentence and specific supporting sentences, and a concluding paragraph that summarizes the body paragraph.

Look at the ideas one writer gathered for an essay on her favorite pastime:

cooking and canning

make delicious jelly and jam

make lots of tomato sauce

make great presents

garden vegetables all winter long

cheap

relaxing to do such an old-fashioned pastime

Look at how she organized the ideas into a three-paragraph essay:

_____

I am a busy person because I work a very demanding job and have two kids. I do a lot of things to relax. I love to knit and sew in the winter, and in the summer I work in my garden. However, my favorite pastime is canning fruit and vegetables from my garden. I love canning because it is a relaxing, old-fashioned pastime that results in plenty of delicious, inexpensive food for my family.

_____

Canning is an old-fashioned way to relax and prepare good, inexpensive food for my family. I love getting together with my two aunts to can food from our gardens. We get together several times during summer to can fruits and vegetables. Canning is an old-fashioned custom we learned from my great-grandmother, who canned on her farm in Arkansas. We can delicious fruit and vegetables, like jelly, jam, corn relish, and tomato sauce. Everything is delicious, and it's very cheap. Then my family can enjoy delicious, healthful foods from my garden all fall and winter. I also give my homemade jelly and jam to friends as gifts.

I think you will agree that canning is a great hobby. It's fun and the products are delicious. I always look forward to summer so I can do more canning. I cannot wait until my daughter Samantha is old enough to help me during canning season.

EXERCISE 7

Directions: Look again at the three-paragraph essay on canning. Respond to the following statements.

1. Which paragraph is the introduction? the body? the conclusion? Write *introduction, body,* or *conclusion* on the appropriate line next to each paragraph.

2. Find the thesis statement. Circle it.

3. Find the topic sentence of the body paragraph. Underline it.

4. Find at least one sentence in the conclusion that relates the main idea of the essay to broader ideas. Draw a box around it.

Answers are on page **273.**

LOOKING AT LANGUAGE: *Effective Sentences*

Thesis Statements

In a three-paragraph essay, a good introductory paragraph ends with a **thesis statement**, a statement of what is to follow in the body paragraph.

Read the following introductory paragraph. Circle the thesis statement. Does it give a clear idea of what the paragraph is going to be about? Why do you think so?

> I must say that I really do not practice many sports. I do not like to run, and I really do not like games such as baseball or basketball. However, I know that exercise is an important part of staying healthy. That's why I try to walk as much as possible. Walking is my favorite sport because it's easy to incorporate into my day and provides exercise and relaxation.

The thesis statement is *Walking is my favorite sport because it's easy to incorporate into my day and provides exercise and relaxation.* If you said that it does in fact give a clear idea of what the body paragraph is going to be about, you are correct. The body paragraph is going to give information on why walking is an easy way to get exercise and to relax.

EXERCISE 8

Directions: Circle the letter of the best thesis statement for each paragraph below.

1. I love holidays. Picnics are fun on Labor Day and the Fourth of July. I also enjoy giving my friends candy on Valentine's Day.

   a. But my favorite holiday is Thanksgiving because of all the food and family togetherness.

   b. Thanksgiving is another important holiday.

2. Some people say that the best things in life are free. I am not so sure.

   a. Old sayings are never very accurate.

   b. This is because many important things, like love, do not cost money, but require a lot of energy and effort.

Answers are on page 274.

Topic Sentences

A good body paragraph begins with a **topic sentence** that is a restatement of the thesis statement. Read the body paragraph for the essay on walking. Does it have a topic sentence?

> On nice days I simply walk to work. I also walk as much as possible while shopping. If I am going to the mall, I try to park far from the mall entrance and then walk to the door, in order to get exercise. I always take the stairs rather than the elevator or escalator at work and at the mall. That way I get some extra exercise, too. I use the extra time to relax my mind and think peaceful thoughts or to plan my free time. That way, I can relax a little. One day I figured that if I walk to work three times a week, park far from store entrances, and always take the stairs, I get about five hours of exercise a week. That is pretty good—and it helps me keep my weight down and my muscles strong.

If you answered that this paragraph does not have a topic sentence, you are correct. Now look at the possible topic sentences and choose the best one:

(a) I like walking because it's an easy way to get some relaxation and exercise.

(b) Walking is fun.

(c) Walking up and down stairs helps me build muscles.

If you chose sentence (a), you are correct. This sentence restates the thesis statement and gives a good indication of the content of the body paragraph. Sentence (b) is too general to be a topic sentence, and sentence (c) is too specific—it could be another supporting sentence in the body paragraph.

EXERCISE 9

Directions: Read the following body paragraphs. Write a topic sentence for each one.

1. _____ .
First you heat a cup of milk. Then pour it into a mug. Add a teaspoon of chocolate syrup and stir.

2. _____ .
The Grand Canyon is more than a mile deep. It's about 217 miles long and about 18 miles wide. When people see it they cannot believe it!

3. _____ .
I Love Lucy is really funny because of all the misadventures Lucy gets into. She is always trying to fool her husband or figure out a way to meet a famous star. She wears hilarious disguises and gets into all sorts of trouble.

Answers are on page 274.

1. Which sentence below would be most effective at the end of paragraph A?

   (1) On-the-job training is very important to everyone.
   (2) For this reason, PricePlus offers a great on-the-job training program to help employees in all areas of the company grow their skills.
   (3) The business math course is the most beneficial for people who want a promotion to cashier manager.
   (4) The company also offers regular raises and bonuses after each year of employment.
   (5) The company is doing this because there have been a lot of complaints lately.

2. Which sentence below would be most effective at the beginning of paragraph B?

   (1) The most important training courses are in customer service.
   (2) All of our training courses are excellent.
   (3) There are many reasons why everyone should take a training course at least once a year.
   (4) Here are a few examples to help you understand the training opportunities available to help you become the best worker possible.
   (5) We offer over 50 different training courses.

3. Which revision would make paragraph C more effective?

   (1) Move sentence 12 to the end of paragraph B
   (2) Move sentence 12 to follow sentence 13
   (3) Remove sentence 12
   (4) Move sentence 15 to follow sentence 12
   (5) Remove sentence 15

Answers are on page 274.

WRITING A GED ESSAY: *The Three-Paragraph Essay*

- A three-paragraph essay has room for more information and detail than a one-paragraph essay.

A three-paragraph essay has an introductory paragraph, a body paragraph, and a concluding paragraph.

- A three-paragraph essay allows more opportunities for presenting the topic in the introductory paragraph and for relating it to broader ideas in the concluding paragraph.

- The introductory paragraph of a three-paragraph essay is organized from general to specific, and it ends with a thesis statement, which indicates the contents of the body paragraph.

- The body paragraph gives specific facts and details to back up the thesis statement. The body paragraph usually begins with a topic sentence, which restates the thesis statement and indicates the organization of the body paragraph.

- The concluding paragraph is organized from specific to general. It sums up the main ideas in the body paragraph and relates them to broader issues.

- The sentences in a good three-paragraph essay should all be written in the same tone.

GED Practice

Directions: Use the four steps of the writing process to create a three-paragraph essay that responds to the following GED essay topic. Follow the steps below.

TOPIC

What is your favorite sport or pastime? Why do you like it?

In your essay, state your favorite sport or pastime. Give specific reasons about why you like it. Use your personal observations, experience, and knowledge.

---

1. Gather Ideas

Read the essay topic and think of the main idea for your three-paragraph essay. Write your main idea on the line below. Use the space on the next page to gather ideas using an idea map or idea list.

Main idea: _____

Gather your ideas here.

2. **Organize Your Ideas**

   A. Review your idea map or list. Use the following checklist. Add missing information and cross off extra information.

       1. ☐ My idea map or list gives specific details.

       2. ☐ All the ideas back up the main idea. Cross off any ideas that are not relevant.

   B. Decide the order you will use to write your essay. Number the ideas in this order.

3. **Write Your Essay**

   Use your idea map or list to write a good three-paragraph essay on a separate sheet of paper. Use the essay diagram on page 92 to help you structure your essay. Do not spend a lot of time worrying about grammar, punctuation, or spelling. You will check for mistakes after you write your essay.

4. Revise Your Essay

A. Check your essay's ideas and organization using the following list.

1. ☐ My introductory paragraph is organized from general to specific and ends with a thesis statement.

2. ☐ My body paragraph begins with a topic sentence that accurately sums up what the paragraph is about.

3. ☐ All the sentences in my body paragraph back up the main idea.

4. ☐ My concluding paragraph is organized from specific to general.

5. ☐ My concluding paragraph sums up the main idea of the essay and relates it to broader issues.

B. Check your essay for standards of Edited American English.

1. ☐ My sentences begin with capital letters and end with periods.

2. ☐ My words are spelled correctly.

3. ☐ My paragraphs are indented.

4. ☐ My sentences are written in the correct tone.

Answers are on page 274.

Writing and Life

Directions: Use the four steps of the writing process to create a three-paragraph essay that responds to the following essay topic. Write your essay on a separate sheet of paper.

─────────── **T O P I C** ───────────

What can people do to have a more healthful diet?

In your essay, state what people can do to have a more healthful diet. Give reasons to back up your views. Use your personal observations, experience, and knowledge.

Answers are on page 274.

Self-Assessment

Part A

Directions: Ask your instructor or a friend to review your work on page 103, or review it yourself. Answer the following questions. Write **yes** or **no** on the appropriate lines below.

1. _____ Is the introductory paragraph organized from general to specific, and does it end with a thesis statement?

2. _____ Does the body paragraph begin with a topic sentence that accurately sums up what the paragraph is about?

3. _____ Do all of the sentences in the body paragraph back up the main idea?

4. _____ Is the concluding paragraph organized from specific to general?

5. _____ Does the concluding paragraph sum up the main idea of the essay and relate it to broader issues?

6. _____ Do the sentences in the essay begin with capital letters and end with periods?

7. _____ Are the words in the essay spelled correctly?

8. _____ Are the paragraphs in the essay indented?

Part B

Directions: Based on your answers to Part A, respond to the statements below.

1. Name a new strength in your writing that you want to continue to use in future assignments.

   _____

2. Name a feature of your writing that you want to improve by reviewing the information in Chapter 6.

   _____

Answers are on page 274.

CHAPTER 7

Cause and Effect

Cause and effect is another common way to answer a GED essay topic. Causes are the reasons for something. Effects are the results of something. Read the following essay topic and cause-and-effect essay.

—————————— T O P I C ——————————

Why do traffic accidents happen?

In your essay, explain why traffic accidents occur. Use your personal observations, experience, and knowledge.

It seems like there is an accident on the corner near the supermarket where I shop almost every day. In fact, our local newspaper says that the number of accidents is up over last year. Why are there so many accidents? There are at least three reasons for the rise in accidents in our town.

Accidents are up because drivers hurry too much, drivers talk on cell phones, and traffic is too heavy. First, most of the accidents seem to happen during rush hour. People are hurrying to get to work or to get home. They drive too fast and don't pay attention. Suddenly, crash! An accident! Second, I think that too many people are talking on cell phones when they drive. As a result, they do not pay attention and suddenly find themselves in an accident. Most important, there is simply too much traffic. At work we noticed that accidents went up when the new movie theater opened next door. More people were coming to the shopping center, and suddenly we started noticing more accidents in the parking lot and the streets nearby. In fact, accidents have increased all over town. That's because so many people have moved here and increased traffic.

Rushing, talking on the phone, and having too much traffic are the causes of the rise of accidents in our town. To cut down on the number of accidents, people need to slow down, cut down on cell phone use, and drive less. Then our town will be safer for everybody.

Answer the following questions:

1. What is the main idea of the essay?

2. Is the essay mainly about causes or effects?

3. What are the causes of accidents according to the writer?

4. Is the essay convincing? Does the writer give enough information to support the main idea?

LEARNING TO WRITE: *A Cause-and-Effect Essay*

A **cause** makes something happen. An **effect** is the result of something that happened first. The cause always happens first. The effect is its result. Look at the following example:

<u>She hit the brakes too late.</u> <u>She smashed into the car in front of her.</u>
         CAUSE   **EFFECT**

In this example she got into an accident (the effect) because she did not brake in time (the cause).

EXERCISE 1

Part A

Directions: What is the cause and what is the effect in each sentence below? Write **C** above every cause and **E** above every effect.

1. They got home very late, and they couldn't find a parking space.

2. He got into an accident because he was driving too fast.

3. He got really angry and yelled at the driver of the other car.

4. She wasn't paying attention and ran a red light.

5. He got completely lost after he made a wrong turn.

Part B

Directions: Complete the chart below with appropriate causes and effects.

Cause	Effect
1. He was driving too fast.	1.
2.	2. They got fat.
3. She left her wallet at home.	3.
4.	4. He had to take his car to the body shop.
5.	5. They were really tired.

Answers are on page 274.

When you write about cause and effect, you usually write about either causes or effects. Look at the following essay topics. For which one would you write mainly about causes? effects? Write *causes* or *effects* on the appropriate line.

1. _____ Why are more and more young people starting to smoke?

2. _____ What is the impact of smoking on young people's health?

If you said that an essay on the first question would be mainly about causes and an essay on the second topic would be mainly about effects, you are correct. The first question asks for causes (why young people are smoking). The second topic asks for effects (what happens when young people smoke).

Often a key phrase in the essay topic will alert you to whether your essay should focus on causes or effects. Look at the following chart:

Phrases That Signal Causes	Phrases That Signal Effects
what is the cause of	what are the results of
give reasons why	what happens when
explain why	what happens after
why	what is the impact of

EXERCISE 2

Directions: For each essay question below, circle the key words or phrases that indicate cause or effect. Then write **cause** or **effect** on the line.

1. _____ What are the reasons that people overeat?

2. _____ Why do people spend so much time watching TV?

3. _____ Why do some people run up high credit card debt?

Answers are on page 274.

A cause-and-effect essay should follow the normal organization of an essay. A three-paragraph essay, such as the one on page 106, should have an introductory paragraph, a body paragraph, and a concluding paragraph. The introductory paragraph should have a thesis statement, and the body paragraph should have a topic sentence.

EXPANDING IDEAS: *T-Charts*

A **T-chart** is a good way to gather ideas for a cause-and-effect essay. A T-chart is a simple, two-column chart that looks like a *T*. The first column is labeled *cause* and the second column is labeled *effect*.

Cause	Effect

Look at the T-chart the writer made for the essay on accidents.

Cause	Effect
people talk on the phone while driving	the number of accidents has gone up
people hurry too much	
traffic has increased	

Can you add an additional cause to the T-chart?

EXERCISE 3

Directions: Respond to the statements below.

1. Read the following GED essay topic. Circle the key words and phrases that tell you whether you will write mainly about causes or effects.

────────────── **TOPIC** ──────────────

Why do so many people drive instead of taking public transportation?

In your essay, state the reasons why people do not use public transportation. Use your personal observations, experience, and knowledge.

2. What will you mainly write about?
   Write **causes** or **effects** on the line. _____

3. Gather ideas for a GED essay. Complete the following T-chart.

Cause	Effect

Order of Importance

After you have gathered your ideas, you need to put them in order. A good way to order your ideas in a cause-and-effect essay is **order of importance**. You can order from most important to least important. Or you can order from least important to most important. Usually, ordering from least important to most important is better because that way your body paragraph ends with your strongest idea. That will leave a lasting impression on the reader. Number your ideas in the order in which you will write about them. Look at how the writer of the essay on accidents ordered the ideas below:

Cause	Effect
② people talk on the phone while driving	the number of accidents has gone up
① people hurry too much	
③ traffic has increased	

EXERCISE 4

Directions: Look at the T-chart you created in Exercise 3. Number the ideas in the order in which you will use them.

Answers are on page | **274.**

LOOKING AT LANGUAGE: *Sentence Combining*

Compound Sentences

When you write about cause and effect, you can put the cause and the effect in two different sentences:

> She didn't hit the brakes in time. She hit the car in front of her.

How might you combine these sentences? Here are some possibilities:

> She didn't hit the brakes in time, and she hit the car in front of her.

> She didn't hit the brakes in time, so she hit the car in front of her.

Both of these longer sentences use **coordinating conjunctions** (*so* and *and*) to join the smaller sentences. Common coordinating conjunctions include *and, but, yet, or, nor, for,* and *so.* Of these coordinating conjunctions, *and, for,* and *so* are often used to join sentences that state causes and effects.

The two smaller sentences became clauses in the larger sentence. A **clause** is a group of words with a subject and verb that is part of a larger sentence. Because each clause in the preceding example can stand alone as a sentence, the clauses are called **independent clauses.** Two independent clauses joined by a conjunction is called a **compound sentence.**

When you use a coordinating conjunction to join independent clauses, you must use a comma between the clauses.

> She was driving very quickly, for she was late for a doctor's appointment.

EXERCISE 5

Directions: Use coordinating conjunctions to join the sentences below. Don't forget to use a comma.

1. He was talking on his cell phone. He got into an accident.

_____

2. Mr. Williams was driving too quickly. He got a speeding ticket.

_____

3. She can't drive any more. Her driver's license has expired.

_____

Answers are on page 274.

Complex Sentences

Look again at the following cause and effect:

She didn't hit the brakes in time. She hit the car in front of her.

Now look at how the writer joined the sentences this time:

She hit the car in front of her because she didn't hit the brakes in time.

The conjunction *because* joins the two clauses. Notice that the second clause *(because she didn't hit the brakes in time)* cannot stand alone as a sentence. For this reason it is called a **dependent clause**. Look at the first clause *(She hit the car in front of her)*. Is it independent or dependent?

If you answered independent, you are right. It can stand alone as a sentence.

A **complex sentence** consists of an independent clause and a dependent clause joined by a conjunction. The conjunctions that join the clauses in complex sentences are called **subordinating conjunctions**. Common subordinating conjunctions include *when, while, although, because, since, so that,* and *in order that.* Of these, *because, since, so that,* and *in order that* are often used to show cause and effect.

When the dependent clause comes first in a complex sentence, use a comma after the dependent clause. If the independent clause comes first, do not use a comma.

EXERCISE 6

Directions: Complete each sentence with a dependent clause that makes sense. Add a comma if necessary, and be sure to use a subordinating conjunction.

1. He got home late ————————————————.

2. ———————————————— they had to work overtime.

3. We have to get up early tomorrow ————————————————.

4. ———————————————— the train was late.

5. I got a bonus ————————————————.

Answers are on page 274.

Run-on Sentences, Comma Splices, and Fragments

A **run-on sentence** consists of two clauses that are not joined with a conjunction. Look at the following examples. Which is a run-on sentence?

He got up early he wanted to go for a run in the park.

He took a shower, and he got ready for work.

If you said that the first sentence is a run-on, you are correct. To fix the run-on, add a conjunction (and a comma, if necessary).

He got up early **because** he wanted to go for a run in the park.

A **comma splice** is similar to a run-on. It consists of two clauses joined only by a comma. Which of these sentences is a comma splice?

He got up early, he could go for a run.

He got up early, so he could go for a run.

If you said the first sentence is a comma splice, you are correct. To fix a comma splice, add a conjunction (and a comma, if necessary).

A dependent clause cannot stand alone as a sentence. A dependent clause that stands along is called a **fragment**. Which of these is a fragment?

Because he needed to earn some extra spending money for the holidays.

Because his old truck broke down, he bought a new one.

If you said that the first item is a fragment, you are correct. One way to fix this error is to delete the word *because:*

He needed to earn some extra money for the holidays.

Another way to fix this fragment is to join it to another clause:

He got a part-time job because he needed to earn some extra money for the holidays.

EXERCISE 7

Part A

Directions: What is wrong with the phases below? Write **R** for run-on, **C** for comma splice, or **F** for fragment.

1. _____ Since he didn't have a car.

2. _____ They went to the store, they needed milk and eggs.

3. _____ The car broke down it ran out of oil.

4. _____ Ms. Pulaski studied every night she wanted to pass the GED Test.

5. _____ Because he loved his job.

Part B

Directions: Rewrite the phrases above correctly. Add a conjunction to the run-ons and the comma splices. Add an independent clause to the fragments. Be sure to use a comma where necessary.

1. _____

_____

2. _____

_____

3. _____

_____

4. _____

_____

5. _____

_____

Answers are on page 274.

GED Connection

Directions: Choose the one best answer to each question.

Dear Guest,

(A)

(1) On behalf of all of our employees, I would like to welcome you to the Holiday Hotel at Magicland Amusement Park! (2) Because we value all of our guests. (3) We want to do everything to make your visit to Magicland a memorable experience. (4) Here are a few things that will make your stay a little more enjoyable. (5) Our hotel offers three great services for visitors to Magicland.

(B)

(6) First, our free courtesy shuttle to Magicland starts at 9:00 a.m. and ends at 11:00 P.M. (7) Many families want to take the shuttle. (8) You should make reservations with the shuttle desk. (9) Second, the restaurants in Magicland are very expensive. (10) You should consider coming back to the hotel for lunch. (11) Our shuttle can pick you up at the Magicland gate for a relaxing lunch in our dining room. (12) After lunch, your kids can take a nap they will be ready for an afternoon of fun at Magicland. (13) Finally, lines are long at the Magicland ticket office. (14) We sell discount tickets at the front desk. (15) You can save time and money.

(C)

(16) If there is anything else we can do to make your stay more enjoyable, please contact me or any member of the hotel staff at extension 2257.

Sincerely,

Francisco Delgadillo,
General Manager
Holiday Hotel at Magicland

1. **Sentences 2 and 3: Because we value all of our <u>guests. We</u> want to do everything to make your visit to Magicland a memorable experience.**

   Which is the best way to write the underlined portion of the text? If the original is the best way, choose option (1).

   (1) guests. We
   (2) guests, we
   (3) guests we
   (4) guests so we
   (5) guests and we

2. **Sentence 5: Our hotel offers three great services for visitors to Magicland.**

   Which revision would make paragraph B more effective?

   (1) move sentence 5 to the beginning of paragraph B
   (2) move sentence 5 to the end of paragraph B
   (3) move sentence 5 to follow sentence 3
   (4) move sentence 5 to follow sentence 7
   (5) remove sentence 5

3. **Sentences 7 and 8: Many families want to take the shuttle. You should make reservations with the shuttle desk.**

   The most effective combination of sentences 7 and 8 would include which group of words?

   (1) Many families want to take the shuttle since you
   (2) Many families want to take the shuttle, you
   (3) Since you should make reservations with the shuttle desk, many families
   (4) Although many families want to take the shuttle, you
   (5) Many families want to take the shuttle, so you

4. **Sentence 12: After lunch, your kids can take a <u>nap they</u> will be ready for an afternoon of fun at Magicland.**

   Which is the best way to write the underlined portion of the text? If the original is the best way, choose option (1).

   (1) nap they
   (2) nap, they
   (3) nap, so they
   (4) nap, but they
   (5) nap because they

Answers are on page 275.

WRITING A GED ESSAY: *Cause and Effect*

- Cause and effect is a common way to answer a GED essay topic.

- A cause makes something happen. An effect is the result of something that happened first.

- A cause-and-effect essay usually focuses on causes or on effects.

- A T-chart is a good way to gather ideas for a cause-and-effect essay.

- The coordinating conjunctions, *and, for,* and *so* are often used to join sentences that state causes and effects.

- The subordinating conjunctions *because, since, so that,* and *in order that* are often used to join sentences that state causes and effects.

- Run-ons can be avoided by adding a comma and a coordinating conjunction to join the two clauses.

- Comma splices can be avoided by adding a coordinating conjunction after the comma to join the two clauses.

- Fragments consisting of a single dependent clause can be avoided by joining the clause to an independent clause with a subordinating conjunction.

GED Practice

Directions: Use the four steps of the writing process to create a three-paragraph cause-and-effect essay that responds to the following GED essay topic. Follow the steps below.

--- T O P I C ---

Why do traffic accidents happen?

In your essay, explain why traffic accidents occur. Give reasons to back up your views. Use your personal observations, experience, and knowledge.

1. Gather Ideas

Read the essay topic and think of the main idea for your three-paragraph essay. Write your main idea on the line below. Decide whether your essay will focus on causes or effects. Then gather ideas using the T-chart on the following page.

Main idea: _____

Will you mainly write about causes or effects?

_____

Cause	Effect

2. Organize Your Ideas

A. Review the ideas in your T-chart. Use the following checklist.

  1. ☐ My T-chart gives specific causes and effects.

  2. ☐ All of my ideas back up the main idea.

B. Decide the order you will use to write your essay. Number the ideas in that order.

3. Write Your Essay

Use your ordered T-chart to write a good three-paragraph essay. Do not spend a lot of time worrying about grammar, punctuation, or spelling. You will check for mistakes after you write your essay. Write your essay on a separate sheet of paper.

4. Revise Your Essay

A. Check your essay's ideas and organization using the following list.

1. ☐ All my ideas back up or support the main idea of the essay.

2. ☐ My essay focuses on causes or effects.

3. ☐ My essay has an introductory paragraph, body paragraph, and concluding paragraph.

4. ☐ My introduction has a thesis statement.

5. ☐ My body paragraph has a topic sentence.

B. Check your essay for standards of Edited American English.

1. ☐ I used coordinating conjunctions to join independent clauses.

2. ☐ I used subordinating conjunctions to join dependent and independent clauses.

3. ☐ I avoided run-ons by adding a comma and a coordinating conjunction to join the two clauses.

4. ☐ I avoided fragments consisting of a single dependent clause by joining them to an independent clause.

Answers are on page 275.

Writing and Life

Directions: Use the four steps of the writing process to create a three-paragraph essay that responds to the following essay topic. Write your essay on a separate sheet of paper.

─────────────── **TOPIC** ───────────────

Not all citizens exercise their right to vote. What are the causes of voter apathy?

In your essay, give reasons why not all people vote. Use your personal observations, experience, and knowledge.

Answers are on page 275.

Self-Assessment

Part A

Directions: Ask your instructor or a friend to review your work on page 121, or review it yourself. Answer the following questions. Write **yes** or **no** on the appropriate lines below.

1. _____ Do all of the ideas back up or support the main idea of the essay?

2. _____ Does the essay focus on causes or effects?

3. _____ Does the essay have an introductory paragraph, body paragraph, and concluding paragraph?

4. _____ Does the introduction have a thesis statement?

5. _____ Does the body paragraph have a topic sentence?

6. _____ Are coordinating conjunctions used to join independent clauses?

7. _____ Are subordinating conjunctions used to join dependent and independent clauses?

8. _____ Are commas and coordinating conjunctions added to run-ons to join independent clauses?

9. _____ Are fragments consisting of a single dependent clause joined to an independent clause?

Part B

Directions: Based on your answers to Part A, respond to the statements below.

1. Name a new strength in your writing that you want to continue to use in future assignments.

   _____

2. Name a feature of your writing that you want to improve by reviewing the information in Chapter 7.

   _____

Answers are on page 275.

CHAPTER 8
Narration

Narration is a very common writing pattern. When you narrate, you talk about events that happened in the past. Read the following essay topic and narrative essay.

TOPIC

What has been the happiest day of your life so far?

In your essay, tell what happened on the happiest day of your life. Explain what happened that made it so wonderful. Use your personal observations, experience, and knowledge.

I have had many wonderful experiences during my life. Getting married was a real highlight. So was the day that I won $500 in the lottery. However, for me the happiest day of my life was the day I took my two precious sons, Kevin and Anthony, to Disneyland. We enjoyed every minute of our visit.

We had fun from morning until night. We got to the park bright and early. As soon as the gates opened, we went in and went to the rides. We rode on three rides in the first hour! Kevin and Anthony screamed and laughed on every ride! It was so wonderful to see them having so much fun. They said that their favorite ride was the Pirates of the Caribbean. After lunch, we took the Monorail back to our hotel, and the boys took short naps. While they were sleeping, I wrote postcards. After they got up, we went back to the park. We saw Minnie and Mickey and took pictures with them. Kevin was so cute! He was a little afraid of Mickey at first, but he really liked Minnie. Then we rode on the Jungle Cruise, an enjoyable ride down a river. Next, we went to Cinderella's Castle. That night, we saw a parade with two great marching bands. Then the fireworks started. After the fireworks, we got ice cream cones. After we finished our ice cream, we took the Monorail back to our hotel. My sons fell asleep as soon as their heads hit their pillows.

It was wonderful to have so much fun with my two beautiful sons. After we got home, we could not wait until our pictures were ready. I hope that I can save up enough money to take my precious sons to Disneyland again next year!

Answer the following questions:

1. Where did the family go?

2. What was their favorite ride?

3. What did they do right after lunch?

4. Which did they do first, watch the parade or see the fireworks?

5. What's the last thing they did before they left Disneyland for the night?

LEARNING TO WRITE: *A Narrative Essay*

Narrative writing allows you to write about something that happened in the past. A GED essay topic might ask you to write about a personal experience that happened in the past. Which of the following topics would most likely require you to write a narrative essay?

1. What is your favorite means of transportation for a long trip? Why?

2. What is the nicest trip you have every gone on? Why was it so nice?

If you chose the second topic, you are correct. This topic asks you to talk about a series of events that happened in the past—in this case, a nice trip that you took. The first topic asks you to give reasons why you prefer one means of transportation. In this case, you would most likely write a descriptive essay.

EXERCISE 1

Directions: Look at each GED essay topic below. Which type of essay would you most likely write? Choose from the following list, and write the appropriate type on the line next to each topic.

Cause and effect   Description   Narration   Process

1. _____ What's your favorite kind of weather?

2. _____ What's the scariest experience you've ever had?

3. _____ How do you cook a hot dog?

4. _____ Why do so many people eat food high in fat despite health warnings?

5. _____ What did you do last weekend?

6. _____ What is tallest building you've ever been in? What is the view like from the top?

7. _____ What are the risks of drinking and driving?

8. _____ How do you pitch a tent when you're camping?

Answers are on page 275.

Chronological Order

When you narrate, you describe events in the order in which they happened. The name of this order is **chronological order**. Look at the events below. Are they in chronological order?

> I took a shower.
>
> I got up at 5:00 A.M.

If you said that the events are not in chronological order, you are correct. They are out of order. The person had to get up before taking a shower.

EXERCISE 2

Directions: Look at the following list of events from the essay on page 124. Put them in chronological order. Write numbers from **1** (first) to **5** (last).

a. _____ We rode on the Pirates of the Caribbean.

b. _____ We took our pictures with Minnie and Mickey.

c. _____ We entered the park.

d. _____ We watched the parade.

e. _____ Kevin and Anthony took naps.

Answers are on page 275.

A narrative essay should have the same structure as any good essay. A one-paragraph essay should have a topic sentence. A good three-paragraph essay should have an introductory paragraph, a body paragraph, and a concluding paragraph. The introductory paragraph should have a thesis statement, and the body paragraph should have a topic sentence.

EXPANDING IDEAS: *Brainstorming*

When you use chronological order, you organize information according to the order in which it happened. A good way to gather and organize ideas in chronological order is **brainstorming**.

When you brainstorm, you list all of your ideas in the order in which you think of them. At this point you do not have to worry about making sure the ideas are in the correct order for writing your essay. Rather, you simply list them. Look at the list the writer made for the essay on the trip to Disneyland.

got to the park early

went in as soon as the gates opened

rode on three rides in the first hour

screaming and laughing

lunch

Monorail to hotel, naps

wrote postcards

back to the park

pictures of Minnie and Mickey

Cinderella's Castle

Jungle Cruise

ice cream cones

parade, bands, fireworks,

Monorail back to hotel

kids tired

favorite morning ride—Pirates of the Caribbean

went shopping at mall the next day

Notice that the writer only used brief words and phrases. She did not worry about writing complete sentences at this point, but rather on getting as many good ideas as possible. More important, notice that the writer did not worry about making sure that the ideas were in the right order. She just made sure the ideas were down on paper.

EXERCISE 3

Directions: Read the following GED essay topic. Then use brainstorming to create a list of ideas.

─────────────── **T O P I C** ───────────────

What did you do last weekend?

Write an essay in which you state what you did last weekend.

────────────────────────────────────

_____

_____

_____

_____

_____

_____

_____

_____

_____

_____

_____

_____

_____

_____

_____

_____

_____

_____

Answers are on page 275.

After brainstorming, you need to number your ideas in the order in which they happened. While numbering in order, you can check to make sure that all the ideas are relevant and cross off any irrelevant ideas. Look at the writer's numbered list for the essay on the trip to Disneyland:

1. got to the park early
2. went in as soon as the gates opened
3. rode on three rides in the first hour
4. screaming and laughing
6. lunch
7. Monorail to hotel, naps
9. back to the park
8. wrote postcards
10. pictures of Minnie and Mickey
12. Cinderella's Castle
11. Jungle Cruise
14. ice cream cones
13. parade, bands, fireworks,
15. Monorail back to hotel
16. kids tired
5. favorite morning ride—Pirates of the Caribbean
~~went shopping at mall the next day~~

EXERCISE 4

Directions: Look at the ideas you brainstormed in Exercise 3. Number your ideas in chronological order. Cross off any irrelevant ideas.

Answers are on page 275.

LOOKING AT LANGUAGE: *Time and Sequence*

Simple Past Tense

The **simple past tense** is used for actions that happened at a specific time in the past.

> She arrived at 6 P.M.
>
> She left at 7 P.M.

The simple past tense of regular verbs is formed by adding *ed* or *d* to the base form of the verb.

- Add *d* to regular verbs that end in *e:*

  > bake   baked

- Add *ed* to the base form of all other regular verbs:

  > start   started
  >
  > cook   cooked

- For verbs that end in a consonant and *y,* change the *y* to *i* and add *ed:*

  > study   studied

- For verbs that end in a vowel and *y,* add *ed:*

  > stay   stayed

- For negatives, use *did not* and the base form of the verb:

  > did not bake
  >
  > did not start
  >
  > did not stay

EXERCISE 5

Directions: Write the correct form of the verb in parentheses on each line below.

1. I _____ *(work)* hard yesterday.

2. I _____ *(type)* six letters for my boss.

3. I _____ *(prepare)* two shipments to our biggest customer.

4. However, I _____ *(not wash)* the delivery van.

5. I _____ *(stay)* late to organize some paperwork.

Answers are on page 275.

English has a number of verbs that are irregular in the simple past tense. These verbs are irregular only in the affirmative. The negative is formed with *did not* and the base form of the verb.

go	went	did not go
buy	bought	did not buy
catch	caught	did not catch

The simple past tense of *be* is *was/were:*

She **was** late yesterday.

They **were** on time this morning.

EXERCISE 6

Directions: Complete each sentence below with the simple past tense form of the verb in parentheses.

1. I _____ *(get)* home from work at 7 P.M. yesterday.

2. I _____ *(eat)* dinner.

3. Then I _____ *(read)* a magazine.

4. After that, I _____ *(write)* a letter to my brother. He is in the military overseas.

5. I _____ *(not go)* to bed until 11:30 P.M.

Answers are on page 275.

Past Continuing Tense

The **past continuing tense** is used for actions that continued in the past.

We were living on Green Street.

She was working at Broadway Convenience Store.

EXERCISE 7

Directions: Complete each sentence below by writing the verb in parentheses in the past continuing tense.

1. She _____ (drive) to work.

2. He _____ (paint) the shed and

   _____ (listen) to the baseball game on the radio.

3. They _____ (watch) TV.

4. I _____ (take) a nap.

5. Larry _____ (work) on his car.

Answers are on page 275.

Adverbs of Time and Sequence

When you narrate, you use a number of **adverbs of time**, such as *yesterday* and *last week,* to indicate when the action happened. You also use **adverbs of sequence**, such as *first, last, then, after that, next,* and *last,* to indicate the order of the past tense actions. Look at the following example. Circle the adverbs of time and sequence.

First, we drove from Chicago to St. Louis. We got there last night. This morning, we left for Dallas. Then we had a flat tire.

If you circled *first, last night, this morning,* and *then,* you are correct. These adverbs of time and sequence tell exactly when these actions happened in the past.

EXERCISE 8

Part A

Directions: Rewrite the following paragraph using adverbs of time and sequence.

> We had fun. We went swimming at a beautiful beach. We went to an exciting amusement park. We ate dinner at a fabulous seafood restaurant.

_____

_____

_____

_____

Part B

Directions: Write a paragraph about what you did last weekend. Be sure to use adverbs of time and sequence.

_____

_____

_____

_____

_____

_____

_____

Answers are on page 275.

Combining Related Sentences

Look at the following sentences:

I clocked out of work.

I went to the mall.

Now look at how the writer joined them into a larger sentence:

After I clocked out of work, I went to the mall.

As you learned in Chapter 7, a complex sentence has two clauses: a dependent clause and an independent clause. In the complex sentence above, the first clause *(After I clocked out of work)* is the dependent clause. The other clause *(I went to the mall)* is the independent clause. Words such as *when, while, before,* and *after* are examples of subordinating conjunctions used to join two clauses. Sentences with **subordinating conjunctions** are very common in narrative essays because they show the relationship among past events. Study the following examples:

After we ate lunch, the boys took naps.

I wrote postcards while they were sleeping.

Remember, if the dependent clause precedes the independent clause, you must separate the two clauses with a comma.

EXERCISE 9

Directions: Use the subordinating conjunction in parentheses to join each pair of sentences below.

1. We were watching the parade. We ate popcorn. *(while)*

   _____

2. We got up. We got ready to go to Disneyland. *(after)*

   _____

3. Kevin and Anthony were playing video games. I sat down and rested. *(while)*

   _____

4. Kevin shook hands with Minnie Mouse. I took his picture. *(when)*

   _____

Answers are on page 275.

GED Connection

Directions: Choose the <u>one best answer</u> to each question.

(1) Last summer I took my twin daughters, Marie and Lisa, and four of their friends to the science museum for their birthday party. (2) We had a wonderful time. (3) The girls were old enough to visit the museum by themselves. (4) So they were visiting the exhibits on space travel, I visited the sections on computer technology. (5) Then we met at the main entrance and went to the exhibits on travel and transportation together. (6) We toured the inside of an old submarine and saw some antique train cars. (7) Before we left the museum, we looked at the gift shop for souvenirs. (8) I bought all of them matching T-shirts. (9) We left the museum. (10) We went to a nearby restaurant for lunch and birthday cake.

1. **Sentence 4: So they were visiting the exhibits on space travel, I visited the sections on computer technology.**

   What correction should be made to sentence 4?

   (1) insert *after* before *they*
   (2) insert *before* before *I*
   (3) insert *while* before *they*
   (4) remove *so*
   (5) no correction is necessary

2. **Sentence 7: Before we left the museum, we looked at the gift shop for souvenirs.**

   If you rewrote sentence 7 beginning with

   We left the museum

   The next word should be

   (1) before
   (2) while
   (3) and
   (4) if
   (5) after

3. **Sentences 9 and 10: We left the museum. We went to a nearby restaurant for lunch and birthday cake.**

   The most effective combination of sentences 9 and 10 would include which group of words?

   (1) After we left the museum, we
   (2) While we left the museum, we
   (3) We went to a nearby restaurant for lunch and birthday cake although we
   (4) We left the museum after we
   (5) We left the museum even though we

Answers are on page 275.

WRITING A GED ESSAY: *Narration*

- A GED essay topic might require narration.

- Narration requires chronological (time) order.

- Brainstorming and numbering in order are good ways to gather and organize ideas for an essay in chronological order.

- The simple past tense is used to talk about actions that are completed in the past.

- The past continuing tense is used to talk about actions that continued in the past.

- Adverbs of time and sequence are used to show exactly when actions happened.

- Subordinating conjunctions such as *when*, *while*, *before*, and *after* are used to combine related sentences.

GED Practice

Directions: Use the four steps of the writing process to create a three-paragraph narrative essay that responds to the following GED essay topic. Follow the steps below.

—————————— T O P I C ——————————

What has been the happiest day of your life so far?

In your essay, tell what happened on the happiest day of your life. Explain what happened that made it so wonderful. Use your personal observations, experience, and knowledge.

1. Gather Ideas

Read the essay topic and think of the main idea for your three-paragraph essay. Write your main idea on the line below.

Main idea: _____

On a separate sheet of paper, brainstorm a list of ideas for your essay. Do not worry about writing complete sentences or putting the ideas in chronological order.

2. Organize Your Ideas

Number your ideas in chronological order. Make sure that all the ideas are relevant. Cross off any ideas that are not relevant.

3. Write Your Essay

Use your numbered list to write a good three-paragraph essay on a separate sheet of paper. Do not spend a lot of time worrying about grammar, punctuation, or spelling. You will check for mistakes after you write your essay.

4. Revise Your Essay

A. Check your essay's ideas and organization using the following list.

1. ☐ All of my ideas back up or support the main idea of the essay.

2. ☐ My essay is in chronological order.

3. ☐ My essay has an introductory paragraph, body paragraph, and concluding paragraph.

4. ☐ My introductory paragraph has a thesis statement.

5. ☐ My body paragraph has a topic sentence.

B. Check your essay for standards of Edited American English.

1. ☐ I used the simple past tense and past continuing tenses correctly.

2. ☐ I used adverbs of time and sequence to indicate when actions happened.

3. ☐ I used subordinating conjunctions such as *when, while, before,* and *after* to combine related sentences.

Answers are on page 276.

Writing and Life

Directions: Use the four steps of the writing process to create a three-paragraph essay that responds to the following essay topic. Write your essay on a separate sheet of paper.

——————————— T O P I C ———————————

What did you do at your last big family celebration?

In your essay, state what you did at your last big family celebration. Give specific examples. Use your personal observations, experience, and knowledge.

Self-Assessment

Part A

Directions: Ask your instructor or a friend to review your work on page 137, or review it yourself. Answer the following questions. Write **yes** or **no** on the appropriate line below.

1. _____ Do all of the ideas back up or support the main idea of the essay?

2. _____ Is the essay in chronological order?

3. _____ Does the essay have an introductory paragraph, body paragraph, and concluding paragraph?

4. _____ Does the introduction have a thesis statement?

5. _____ Does the body paragraph have a topic sentence?

6. _____ Are the simple past and past continuing tenses used correctly?

7. _____ Are adverbs of time and sequence used to show when actions happened?

8. _____ Are subordinating conjunctions used to combine related sentences?

Part B

Directions: Based on your answers to Part A, respond to the statements below.

1. Name a new strength in your writing that you want to continue to use in future assignments.

   _____

2. Name a feature of your writing you that want to improve by reviewing the information in Chapter 8.

   _____

Answers are on page 276.

CHAPTER 9

Comparison and Contrast

When you compare and contrast, you look at two different objects, people, places, or ideas. You find out how they are the same and how they are different. Read the following essay topic and comparison-contrast essay.

─────────── T O P I C ───────────

Which makes a better pet, a dog or a cat?

In your essay, state whether you think a dog or a cat makes a better pet. Give examples to back up your opinion. Use your personal observations, experience, and knowledge.

Many people keep pets. The most popular pets are dogs and cats. Cats and dogs are very different in many ways. People often love cats and hate dogs, or vice versa. For me, a dog is a perfect pet.

Dogs have three traits that make them better than cats. First of all, dogs are really friendly and loving. Dogs love to be around people, but cats are very solitary animals. My loving dog, Abby, always greets me by wagging her tail whenever I get home. Second, dogs are very helpful. My dog is an excellent watchdog. Always listening for danger, she paces in front of the door when strangers are near our house. To this day, certain kinds of dogs perform many kinds of work. Dogs herd sheep. Hunting dogs help hunters. Cats, on the other hand, are not very hardworking. The only work that cats do is catch mice. Finally, dogs are fun. They love to play with people and go for walks. Cats only like to play with string.

For these reasons, I will always prefer dogs over cats. I know that many people love their cats, but for me I will always have a dog as a pet.

Answer the following questions:

1. What is the writer comparing and contrasting?

2. What are the main differences between the animals?

3. What are the main similarities between the animals?

4. Do you agree with the author? Why?

5. Which animal would you rather have as a pet? Why?

LEARNING TO WRITE: *A Comparison-Contrast Essay*

Comparative writing allows you to find similarities between two things. **Contrastive writing** allows you to find differences between two things. Look at the following statements. Which one is a comparison? Which one is a contrast?

Cats and dogs are popular pets.

Cats are quiet, but dogs are often noisy.

The first sentence is a comparison. It shows one way that cats and dogs are similar. The second sentence is a contrast. It shows one way cats and dogs are different.

EXERCISE 1

Part A

Directions: Which of the following statements are comparisons? Which are contrasts? Check the appropriate box for each.

Comparison	*Contrast*	
☐	☐	1. Cats and dogs have been domesticated for centuries.
☐	☐	2. Cats are good at catching mice, unlike dogs.
☐	☐	3. Cats and dogs often do not get along with one another.
☐	☐	4. Cats can usually keep themselves clean, but people have to wash their dogs.
☐	☐	5. Usually cats do not like water, but many dogs like to swim.

Part B

Directions: Continue comparing and contrasting cats and dogs. Write one comparison and one contrast on the lines below.

Comparison: _____

Contrast: _____

Answers are on page 276.

When would you use comparison and contrast to write an essay? Look at the topics below. Which topic calls for comparison and contrast?

1. How do you heat up a can of soup?

2. Would you rather live in a large city or a small town? Why?

If you chose the second topic, you are correct. This topic asks you to compare and contrast life in a city and life in a small town. The first topic is about a process—the steps for preparing a certain kind of food.

Often a key phrase in the essay topic will alert you to whether your essay should focus on comparison and contrast. Look at the following chart:

Comparison and Contrast: Key Words and Phrases
Which do you prefer, ...?
What are the advantages and disadvantages of ...?
Which is better, ...?
Where would you rather ...?
Which is easier/harder/more difficult...?

EXERCISE 2

Directions: Read the essay topics below. Circle any key words for comparison and contrast. Then decide whether you would use comparison and contrast to answer each one. Write **yes** on the line if you would. Write **no** on the line if you would not.

1. _____ Where would you rather live, in an apartment or in a house?

2. _____ What did you do last Thanksgiving?

3. _____ Which is better, working days or working nights?

4. _____ What are the advantages and disadvantages of driving to work or taking public transportation?

5. _____ What kind of movies do you like better, comedies or action movies?

Answers are on page 276.

Remember, a comparison-contrast essay should have the same structure as any good one-paragraph or three-paragraph essay.

EXPANDING IDEAS: *Venn Diagrams*

A **Venn diagram** is a good way to gather information for a comparison-contrast essay. Look at the Venn diagram the writer created for the essay on cats and dogs.

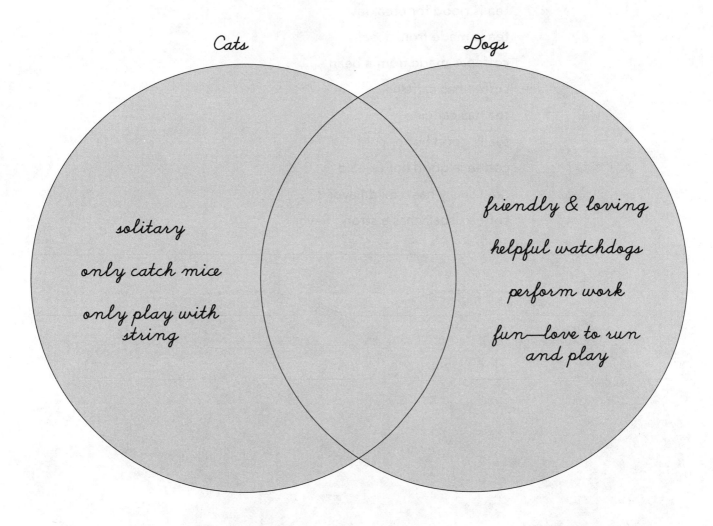

Cats

Dogs

solitary

only catch mice

only play with string

friendly & loving

helpful watchdogs

perform work

fun—love to run and play

As you can see, one circle represents cats, and one circle represents dogs. The area where the circles overlap indicates similarities. The other parts of each circle represent differences. Write the following statement in the appropriate part of the Venn diagram.

Cats and dogs are good companions.

You should have written the statement in the overlapping area, since it is a comparison.

EXERCISE 3

Directions: Look at the following list of ideas. Write the ideas in the appropriate place in the Venn diagram below.

coffee is good for breakfast

tea is good for breakfast

tea is made from a leaf

coffee is made from a bean

coffee has caffeine

tea has caffeine

tea is good hot or cold

coffee is good hot or cold

tea usually has a mild flavor

coffee usually has a strong flavor

Answers are on page 276.

EXERCISE 4

Directions: Read the following GED essay topic. Think of ideas for an essay, and complete the Venn diagram below.

———————————— **TOPIC** ————————————

Which kind of movies do you prefer, comedies or action movies?

In your essay, state whether you prefer comedies or action movies. Give specific reasons to back up your opinion. Use your personal observations, experience, and knowledge.

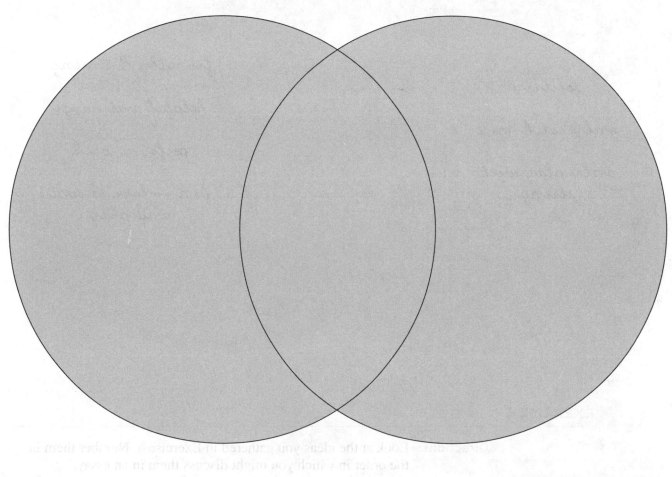

Answers are on page 276.

After you complete your Venn diagram, you need to decide the order in which you will discuss your ideas. You might discuss all the similarities first and then the differences. Or you might discuss each similarity followed by a difference. If there are only similarities or only differences, you still need to decide on the order. No matter how you decide to organize them, you should number the ideas in the order in which you will talk about them. Look at how the writer of the essay on cats and dogs numbered the ideas in the Venn diagram.

Cats   *Dogs*

solitary ②

only catch mice ④

only play with string ⑥

① *friendly & loving*

③ *helpful watchdogs*

perform work

⑤ *fun — love to run and play*

EXERCISE 5

Directions: Look at the ideas you gathered in Exercise 4. Number them in the order in which you might discuss them in an essay.

LOOKING AT LANGUAGE: *Modifying Phrases*

There are several kinds of phrases that can be used to modify another word in a sentence.

Prepositional Phrases

A **prepositional phrase** consists of a preposition and a noun.

> **To this day,** dogs perform many valuable services.

> Cats often look at you **in a condescending manner.**

Always use a comma to set off these phrases when they come at the beginning of a sentence.

> He answered the question **in an angry tone of voice.**

> **In an angry tone of voice,** he answered the question.

Verbal Phrases

A **verbal phrase** uses a verb form to describe a noun. Verbal phrases can end with *ed* or *ing*.

> **Staying beside her owner,** Abby ran through the park.

> **Worried and confused,** the dog howled through the night.

EXERCISE 6

Directions: Add the modifying phrase in parentheses to each sentence below.

1. The skier returned to the lodge. *(hurt in a fall)*

   _____

2. She told the doctor what happened. *(crying and unhappy)*

   _____

3. The doctor told her that her injuries were not serious. *(in a calm voice)*

   _____

4. Her husband helped her to their room to get some rest. *(concerned for her health)*

   _____

Answers are on page 276.

Misplaced Modifiers

Sometimes writers don't place a modifying phrase near the noun it modifies. This modifier is called a **misplaced modifier**. Look at the following sentence. Does it contain a misplaced modifier?

The car hit a tree driving over the curb.

If you said yes, you are correct. The modifier *driving over the curb* is misplaced. The sentence seems to say that the tree was driving, which is impossible. Look at how the writer corrected the sentence:

Driving over the curb, the car hit a tree.

The writer also might correct the misplaced modifier with the following sentence:

The car hit a tree when it drove over the curb.

EXERCISE 7

Directions: Circle the misplaced modifier in each sentence below. Then rewrite the sentence so that the modifier is placed correctly.

1. He gave me my change with a smile.

   _____

2. The dog barked at the car running quickly.

   _____

3. Mr. Maguire arrived at the hospital in an ambulance badly hurt in the car crash.

   _____

4. Under the sofa they couldn't find the flashlight.

   _____

5. The woman finally found her missing dog searching frantically around the neighborhood.

   _____

Answers are on page 276.

Dangling Modifiers

A **dangling modifier** is a modifier that has no clear reference in a sentence.

> Barking wildly, the thief was scared off.

To correct this sentence, you can change the dangling modifier to a dependent clause.

> Because the dog was barking wildly, the thief ran away.

You can also rewrite the sentence entirely.

> Barking wildly, the dog scared off the thief.

EXERCISE 8

Directions: Circle the dangling modifier in each sentence below. Then revise the sentence so it makes sense.

1. Reading the newspaper, time passed quickly.

   _____

2. Closing the door, the keys were locked in the room.

   _____

3. Stuck in traffic, the meeting started.

   _____

4. Entering the supermarket, the produce is on the left.

   _____

5. Entering the room, the furniture was admired.

   _____

Answers are on page 276.

Appositives

An **appositive** is a noun phrase that gives more information about the noun. Appositives are usually set off by commas.

My dog, **Abby,** is a faithful companion.

Max, **my cat,** has a beautiful furry coat.

EXERCISE 9

Directions: Insert the appositive in parentheses into each sentence below. Be sure to use commas to set off the appositive.

1. Frank Ramirez made the announcement. *(the president of the company)*

   _____

2. Maui is part of the Hawaiian Islands. *(a beautiful island)*

   _____

3. My neighbor is really nice. *(Miss Appleby)*

   _____

4. Lake Michigan is one of the largest bodies of water in North America. *(one of the Great Lakes)*

   _____

5. Bert Bowden is taking the GED Test this year. *(a retired bus driver)*

   _____

Answers are on page 276.

GED Connection

Directions: Choose the <u>one best answer</u> to each question.

(A)

(1) Tired and hungry, a pizza sounded like a good idea for dinner. (2) So Mr. Washington called Pizza King his family's favorite pizza restaurant, and ordered an extra-large mushroom and green pepper pizza. (3) The employee told him that the pizza would be there in 30 minutes.

(B)

(4) While waiting for their food, the family decided to fix a large salad. (5) By that time 35 minutes had gone by, and the pizza still was not there. (6) Sitting on the dining room table, the family looked hungrily at the salad. (7) Mr. Washington, ready to eat, said, "Let's have the salad, and by then the pizza will be here." (8) They ate the salad, and still the pizza had not arrived. (9) Finally, Mr. Washington called the restaurant. (10) Then he found out that he had forgotten to give the employee his address. (11) With the correct address, the pizza was delivered.

1. **Sentence 1: Tired and hungry, a pizza sounded like a good idea for dinner.**

    The most effective revision of sentence 1 would begin with which group of words?

    (1) Tired and hungry a pizza sounded
    (2) Tired and hungry, the family thought
    (3) A pizza, tired and hungry,
    (4) For a tired and hungry dinner,
    (5) A pizza sounded tired and hungry

2. **Sentence 2: So Mr. Washington called <u>Pizza King his family's favorite</u> pizza restaurant, and ordered an extra-large mushroom and green pepper pizza.**

    Which is the best way to write the underlined portion of the text? If the original is the best way, choose option (1).

    (1) Pizza King his family's favorite
    (2) Pizza King, his family's favorite
    (3) Pizza King, and his family's favorite
    (4) Pizza King or his family's favorite
    (5) Pizza King being his family's favorite

3. **Sentence 6: Sitting on the dining room table, the family looked hungrily at the salad.**

   If you rewrote sentence 6 beginning with

   The family looked hungrily at the salad

   the next word(s) should be

   (1) sitting on the dining room table
   (2) sitting, on the dining room table
   (3) while sitting on the dining room table
   (4) and the pizza sitting
   (5) and the dining room table

4. **Sentence 11: <u>With the correct address,</u> the pizza was delivered.**

   Which is the best way to write the underlined portion of the text? If the original is the best way, choose option (1).

   (1) With the correct address,
   (2) Having the correct address,
   (3) Soon having the correct address
   (4) As soon as the restaurant had the correct address,
   (5) To get the correct address

Answers are on page 276.

WRITING A GED ESSAY: Comparison and Contrast

- Comparison and contrast indicate the similarities and differences between two things.

- A comparison is a similarity. A contrast is a difference.

- A Venn diagram is a good way to gather ideas for a comparison-contrast essay.

- Prepositional phrases, verbal phrases, and appositives can be used to add additional information to a sentence as long as they are placed correctly.

GED Practice

Directions: Use the four steps of the writing process to create a three-paragraph comparison-contrast essay that responds to the following GED essay topic. Follow the steps below.

——————— T O P I C ———————

Which makes a better pet, a dog or a cat?

In your essay, state whether you think a dog or a cat makes a better pet. Give examples to back up your opinion. Use your personal observations, experience, and knowledge.

1. Gather Ideas

Read the essay topic and think of the main idea for your three-paragraph essay. Write your main idea on the line below.

Main idea: _____

Next, think of ideas for your essay. Complete the Venn diagram below.

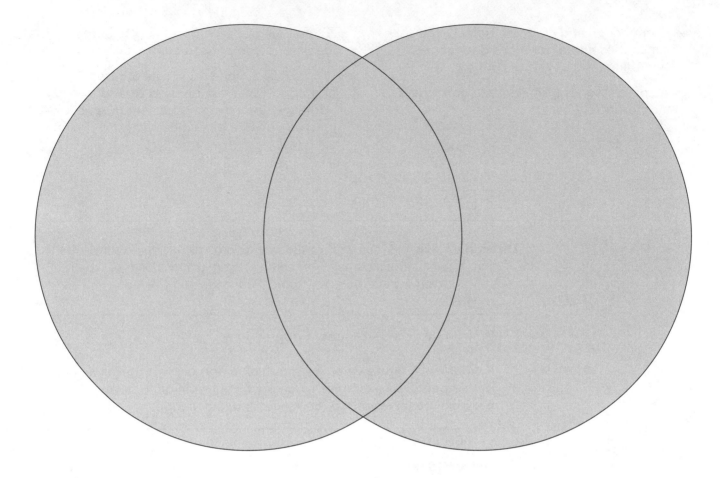

2. Organize Your Ideas

Number your ideas in the order in which you will deal with them in your essay. Make sure that all the ideas are relevant. Cross off any ideas that are not relevant.

3. Write Your Essay

Use your numbered list to write a good three-paragraph essay on a separate sheet of paper. Do not spend a lot of time worrying about grammar, punctuation, or spelling. You will check for mistakes after you write your essay.

4. **Revise Your Essay**

    A. Check your essay's ideas and organization using the following list.

        1. ☐ All of my ideas back up, or support, the main idea of the essay.

        2. ☐ My ideas are in a logical order.

        3. ☐ My essay has an introductory paragraph, body paragraph, and concluding paragraph.

        4. ☐ My introductory paragraph has a thesis statement.

        5. ☐ My body paragraph has a topic sentence.

    B. Check your essay for standards of Edited American English.

        1. ☐ I used prepositional phrases, verbal phrases, and appositives to add additional information.

        2. ☐ I avoided dangling and misplaced modifiers.

        3. ☐ I used commas to set off appositives, initial prepositional phrases, and verbal phrases.

Answers are on page 276.

 # Writing and Life

Directions: Use the four steps of the writing process to create a three-paragraph essay that responds to the following essay topic. Write your essay on a separate sheet of paper.

— T O P I C —

Where is it better to raise kids, a big city or a small town?

In your essay, state whether you think a big city or a small town is a better place to raise kids. Use your personal observations, experience, and knowledge.

Answers are on page 277.

Self-Assessment

Part A

Directions: Ask your instructor or a friend to review your work on page 155, or review it yourself. Answer the following questions. Write **yes** or **no** on the appropriate line below.

1. _____ Do all of the ideas back up or support the main idea of the essay?

2. _____ Is the essay in chronological order?

3. _____ Does the essay have an introductory paragraph, body paragraph, and concluding paragraph?

4. _____ Does the introduction have a thesis statement?

5. _____ Does the body paragraph have a topic sentence?

6. _____ Does the essay avoid dangling modifiers?

7. _____ Does the essay avoid misplaced modifiers?

8. _____ Are appositives used to add additional information?

Part B

Directions: Based on your answers to Part A, respond to the statements below.

1. Name a new strength in your writing that you want to continue to use in future assignments.

   _____

2. Name a feature of your writing that you want to improve by reviewing the information in Chapter 9.

   _____

Answers are on page 277.

CHAPTER 10

The Five-Paragraph Essay

In the previous chapters of this book, you have learned about many different types of writing. You have also practiced writing one-paragraph and three-paragraph essays. Now you are ready to tackle the five-paragraph essay. Read the essay topic and five-paragraph essay below.

TOPIC

What is the nicest experience you have had with your family or friends?

In your essay, describe the nicest experience you have had with your family or friends. Explain why it was so nice. Use your personal observations, experience, and knowledge.

I think it is important to have fun in life, so I always schedule a lot of fun activities with my family and friends. When I found out that my family was going to have a reunion in Chicago, I made sure that I could go. The reunion lasted an entire weekend, and it was fun every minute. There were lots of interesting activities all three days of the reunion.

The reunion began with a fun dinner Friday evening. We all got together at a buffet restaurant. We had a private room for our group. There were almost 70 of us. We ate and talked until the restaurant closed. We had a lot of fun catching up, because many of us had not seen each other for years.

On Saturday we spent the entire day together. In the morning, we met for a boat tour of Chicago. Our tour took us up the Chicago River and then out into the lake. I moved away from Chicago ten years ago, so it was nice to see how the city had changed. There was a lot of talking and laughing as we told stories about different people and places. Then we went to Mulligan's Restaurant for lunch. Mulligan's Restaurant is in our old neighborhood, so all of us had eaten there at one time or another. After that, we went to the Aquarium, where we were able to see fish from all over the world. That night we had a family talent show. There are a lot of talented people in our family, and different relatives played musical instruments, sang, read their poetry, and so on. My sister, Bernice, is a professional dancer in New York, and she performed for us. The youngest performer was my nephew, Dominique, who is five years old. He played a song on a tiny violin.

On Sunday we had a family picnic in the park. Everyone brought food and drinks to share. We visited and enjoyed our meal. Then we had family sports. We played baseball, volleyball, and basketball. One of my cousins plays volleyball at her college, and she taught all the little kids to play. Everyone also brought family pictures, movies, and videos. Some of the photos were almost 100 years old. The oldest thing was a painting of our great, great grandfather. That painting was from 1875! My brother is an Internet genius, and he is going to make a family Web site with all of the pictures, videos, and movies.

As you can see, all three days of our family reunion were wonderful. We renewed our friendships and grew stronger as a family. I hope that we have another great reunion next year.

Answer the following questions:

1. What is the main idea of the essay?

2. Is the essay an example of descriptive writing, narrative writing, or process writing? Why do you think so?

3. What day is the first body paragraph about? The second body paragraph? The third body paragraph?

4. Do you think that the reunion was fun? Why do you think so?

LEARNING TO WRITE: *A Five-Paragraph Essay*

The **five-paragraph essay** is a useful format for writing a good GED essay because it is long enough to explain your ideas adequately in 45 minutes. A five-paragraph essay also has an easy-to-follow organizational structure that will help you score high on the GED Test.

The five-paragraph essay and the three-paragraph essay are very similar in structure. Both have introductory paragraphs with thesis statements, and both have concluding paragraphs.

However, these two essays are different in one key way: A three-paragraph essay has one body paragraph; a five-paragraph essay has three body paragraphs. Each body paragraph in a five-paragraph essay has the same organization as the body paragraph in a three-paragraph essay. It begins with a topic sentence and then provides specific details to back up the topic sentence.

The following Venn diagram sums up the similarities and differences between three-paragraph and five-paragraph essays:

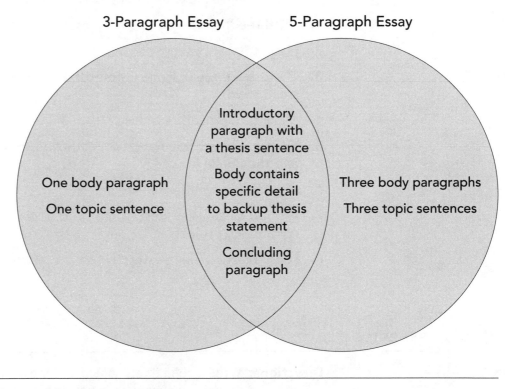

3-Paragraph Essay   5-Paragraph Essay

One body paragraph

One topic sentence

Introductory paragraph with a thesis sentence

Body contains specific detail to backup thesis statement

Concluding paragraph

Three body paragraphs

Three topic sentences

EXERCISE 1

Directions: Look at the essay on pages 157–158. Identify the following parts. Write the letter of the appropriate part next to each paragraph.

a. Introduction
b. Thesis Statement
c. Body Paragraph 1
d. Body Paragraph 2
e. Body Paragraph 3

f. Topic Sentence 1
g. Topic Sentence 2
h. Topic Sentence 3
i. Conclusion

Answers are on page 277.

Writing a Good Thesis Statement

A good introductory paragraph has a thesis statement that explains what the body of the essay will be about. In a five-paragraph essay the thesis statement must indicate what each of the body paragraphs will be about. Look again at the thesis statement from the essay on pages 157–158:

> There were lots of interesting activities all three days of the reunion.

Notice that the thesis statement indicates that the reunion was fun all three days. This is a clear signal to the reader that each of the body paragraphs will be about one of the three days. In fact, the three body paragraphs are about Friday, Saturday, and Sunday.

EXERCISE 2

Directions: Which of the following thesis statements clearly indicates the topic of each body paragraph in a five-paragraph essay? Circle the number of the appropriate statements.

1. My three favorite foods are cheeseburgers, ice cream, and grapes.
2. I love to play basketball.
3. There are three reasons I prefer to live in the city instead of a small town.
4. Making good coffee is easy.
5. To make bread, you need to mix the ingredients, let the dough rise, and then bake it.
6. My dog is a wonderful friend.
7. A good citizen should stay informed, vote, and participate in community projects.
8. I had a terrible day yesterday.

Answers are on page 277.

EXERCISE 3

Directions: Write a good thesis statement for each topic below. Make sure each thesis statement indicates the topic of each body paragraph.

1. What are your favorite ways to spend a rainy Saturday afternoon?

_____

2. Why shouldn't people smoke?

_____

Answers are on page 277.

Writing Good Topic Sentences

When you write a five-paragraph essay, you need to write three good topic sentences, one for each body paragraph. Each topic sentence should be about a different aspect of the thesis statement. Look again at the thesis statement and topic sentences from the essay on pages 157–158:

Thesis Statement	Topic Sentences
There were lots of interesting activities all three days of the reunion.	1. The reunion began with a fun dinner Friday evening. 2. On Saturday, we spent the entire day together. 3. On Sunday we had a family picnic in the park.

Notice that each of the topic sentences focuses on one of the three days mentioned in the thesis statement—Friday, Saturday, and Sunday. In other words, the topic sentences each develop a part of the thesis statement.

EXERCISE 4

Directions: Look at the items you circled in Exercise 2. Choose two of the items and write the thesis statements on the lines below. Then write three good topic sentences to support each thesis statement.

1. Thesis statement: _____

Topic sentence 1: _____

Topic sentence 2: _____

Topic sentence 3: _____

2. Thesis statement: _____

Topic sentence 1: _____

Topic sentence 2: _____

Topic sentence 3: _____

Answers are on page 277.

Making Your Five-Paragraph Essay Interesting

Maintaining reader interest is important, especially in longer essays. One way to create reader interest is in the introduction. Look at these two versions of the introduction to the essay on pages 157–158. Which one is more interesting? Why do you think so?

> I think it is important to have fun in life, so I always schedule a lot of fun activities with my family and friends. When I found out that my family was going to have a reunion in Chicago, I made sure that I could go. The reunion lasted an entire weekend, and it was fun every minute. There were lots of interesting activities all three days of the reunion.

> I did a lot of things last year, and most of them were boring. I don't like my job, and I think that the people in the town where I live are boring and stupid. That's why I decided to go to my family reunion last year in Chicago. The whole weekend was really fun—Friday, Saturday, and Sunday.

If you said that the first version is more interesting, you are correct. It has a positive, upbeat tone. It focuses on something everyone is interested in: having fun. Notice that both introductory paragraphs have good thesis statements. In fact, a good thesis statement is only one part of a good introductory paragraph. Creating interest is also important. Here are some ways to create interest:

- Tell a personal story

> Last year I was walking down the street when I suddenly saw a brand new X100 Mountain Bike. That's when I realized that I wanted to get a bike. Now I ride my bike everywhere. Riding a bike is a fun hobby, a benefit to your health, and a great way to get to work.

- Give an interesting fact

> Every year on February 14, millions of people will exchange Valentines. At the drugstore where I work, we had people waiting in line for more than 15 minutes to buy cards, candy, and flowers for Valentine's Day. People like Valentine's Day because it is a time to show their love to the people they care about most. That's why Valentine's Day is my favorite holiday. I like this holiday because it's a great time to show love for my friends, my family, and my husband.

• Relate the topic to the reader

Imagine that you are driving home after a hard day's work. Suddenly another car careens out of control and hits your front bumper. You get out of your car and then notice that the other driver had been talking on her cell phone just before the accident. Cell phones are a cause of the growing number of accidents on roadways these days. Talking on cell phones while driving should be outlawed in order to cut down on accidents and to save lives and property.

EXERCISE 5

Directions: Read the following topic and introductory paragraph. Write a new introduction that is more interesting.

─────────────── T O P I C ───────────────

Modern technology is significant in the area of human communication.

Write an essay explaining how modern technology has helped people to communicate more effectively.

Nowadays, many people have pagers, cell phones, and wireless e-mail. These devices have changed the way people communicate. Modern technology has helped us communicate more efficiently. Technology lets us stay in contact anywhere, at any time, and in a variety of mediums.

_____

_____

_____

_____

_____

_____

EXPANDING IDEAS: *Essay Diagrams*

In Chapter 6 you were introduced to a graphic organizer that helps you to visualize the structure of a three-paragraph essay. You can use a similar graphic organizer to visualize the structure of a five-paragraph essay.

A good introductory paragraph

• is organized from general to specific.

• states the main idea of the essay.

• ends with a specific thesis statement that tells the reader what to expect in each body paragraph.

Good body paragraphs

• are each about one main idea that supports the main idea of the essay.

• are in the same order as they are mentioned in the thesis statement.

• begin with the topic sentence that states the main idea of the paragraph.

• contain detailed supporting sentences that back up the paragraph's topic sentence.

A good concluding paragraph

• is organized from specific to general.

• begins with a restatement of the thesis statement.

• ends with a general statement that relates the topic of the essay to broader terms.

The essay diagram shows the nature of each paragraph in a five-paragraph essay:

- The introductory paragraph begins with a general statement and builds towards a more specific thesis statement. The introductory paragraph also creates interest in the essay topic.

- The three body paragraphs each begin with a topic sentence, which gives an idea of how the paragraph will be organized. Usually, the topic sentence is a restatement of part of the thesis statement. The rest of each paragraph contains specific supporting sentences to back up the topic sentence.

- The concluding paragraph is organized from specific to general. The first sentence of the concluding paragraph summarizes the main ideas of the body paragraphs, and the rest of the sentences relate these ideas to broader and more general topics.

EXERCISE 6

Directions: What is the role of each part of a five-paragraph essay? Write the letters of the appropriate descriptions on each line. There is more than one letter for each numbered item.

1. _____ Introductory paragraph

2. _____ Body paragraphs

3. _____ Concluding paragraph

a. contains supporting sentences

b. builds interest among readers

c. relates the ideas of the body to broader ideas

d. contains a topic sentence

e. summarizes the ideas in the body paragraphs

f. contains the thesis statement

g. organized from general to specific

h. organized from specific to general

Answers are on page 277.

EXERCISE 7

Part A

Directions: The following paragraphs are in the wrong order. Number them in the correct order from **1** (first) to **5** (last).

a. _____ Mixing the ingredients is the first step. First, I get out flour, water, eggs, salt, and yeast. I measure and mix the ingredients according to the recipe. This is the hardest step because mixing the dough is hard work.

b. _____ What's your favorite food? What really gets your mouth watering? For me, it's homemade bread. I love to bake, so every Saturday morning while my kids are at their swimming lesson, I go into the kitchen and make a batch of homemade bread. The three basic steps are easy—mixing the ingredients, letting the dough rise, and baking the bread.

c. _____ The third step, baking the bread, happens after the dough has risen a second time. I heat the oven and pop in the bread for about 40 minutes. I always watch it carefully. By the time it's done, my kids are home from their swim class. So I always treat them to fresh bread and a bowl of soup.

d. _____ Following all three steps takes all morning. But the end product is a delicious treat that's good for my kids. That's why I always take the time to make bread on Saturdays. It's the little things like this that make life special.

e. _____ The second step, letting the dough rise, is the easiest. I leave the dough in a bowl in a warm place. The yeast reacts with the flour and water, and tiny bubbles begin to form. As the bubbles form, the dough rises. While the dough is rising, I relax, call my friends, or read a book. After about an hour, the dough is ready. Then I form it into a loaf, put it into a pan, and let it rise again.

Part B

Directions: Respond to the statements below.

1. Is this essay an example of a process essay, a narrative essay, or a comparison/contrast essay?

2. Underline the thesis statement.

3. Circle the topic sentences.

Answers are on page 277.

LOOKING AT LANGUAGE: *Paragraph Structure and Organization*

Dividing Paragraphs

A good body paragraph should contain only one main idea. Look at the following paragraph. How many main ideas does it have? What are they? How would you fix the problem?

> Last spring was really wonderful. My family and I went camping in Texas for a week. We went hiking several times and saw some beautiful, rugged scenery. We loved the Texas coast, and we went fishing several times. However, we never caught anything. Then in the winter we went to Florida for Christmas. My parents live there now, so my husband and I and our three kids drove down after school got out. It took two days. We had fun swimming at the beach. We also went to the Everglades. We saw several alligators. We went fishing there, too, because my husband and my father both love to fish. This time we were luckier, and we had fresh fish for dinner almost every night.

If you said that the paragraph has two main ideas, you are correct. The paragraph tells about two wonderful trips—one to Texas and one to Florida. The way to fix the problem is to divide the paragraph into two, so that one paragraph is about the trip to Texas and the other is about the trip to Florida.

EXERCISE 8

Directions: Read the following paragraph. Decide how many paragraphs it should be divided into. Insert a paragraph mark (¶) to show where a new paragraph should begin.

> Williamson Decorating can make your kitchen look great! We can replace the flooring with new vinyl or tile, put in new cabinets, install a new built-in range and dishwasher, and put in a new fridge with an icemaker. Williamson Decorating can also redo your bathroom. We can replace the sink and toilet, spray the bathtub another color, and apply fresh paint or wallpaper. We can also replace all the tile on the floor and walls. We have a selection of beautiful new shower doors that will make any bathroom look brand new.

Answers are on page 277.

Combining Paragraphs

Sometimes a writer unnecessarily creates a new paragraph. If the new paragraph supports the topic sentence of the previous paragraph, the two paragraphs need to be combined. Which of the following paragraphs need to be combined?

(A)

This fall, I was sick twice. In October I caught a cold because I got wet on my way home from work. While I was on the bus, it suddenly began to pour down rain. When I got off the bus, I stepped directly in a deep puddle that soaked my shoes. Since my umbrella was at home, I had no choice but to walk home in the pouring rain.

(B)

By the time I got there I was completely soaked, and I caught a terrible cold. I had a cough, a runny nose, and a sore throat. I was sick for a week and missed two days of work.

(C)

The second time I got sick was in November. I had to work a double shift. I got really tired, and when I got home I had a fever and a sore throat. The next day, I had the flu so bad that I could hardly get out of bed. That time I missed work for a week.

If you said that paragraphs A and B need to be combined, you are correct. These two paragraphs are about the same main idea: the cold the writer caught in October.

EXERCISE 9

Directions: Which of the following paragraphs should be combined? Circle the appropriate letters below.

(A)

I love to ride my bicycle for exercise. I often go to the park to ride, or sometimes I ride my bike when I am taking care of small errands.

(B)

For example, last week, I rode my bike to the bank and the post office. I have a basket for carrying my purse and packages, so I stopped at the supermarket to pick up a few things on my way home.

(C)

I also love to walk in the park for exercise. Sometimes I get up early and walk before the sun comes up. I often see beautiful birds. Once I saw a deer.

(D)

Finally, I love to swim for exercise. I go to the pool near my home on weekends and swim for about half an hour before lunch. I always feel refreshed after a swim.

Answers are on page 277.

Deleting Sentences

Sometimes a writer includes an idea in a paragraph that is irrelevant—not about the main idea. This sentence does not belong in the paragraph and needs to be removed. Read the following paragraph. What is the main idea? Which sentence is not about the main idea?

> Lately I have noticed a number of safety issues that are a hazard for all employees. First, there is no running at any time. Second, all employees in the manufacturing area must wear safety glasses at all times. Operators of drill presses must wear goggles. We need to organize the tools in the woodworking area. Third, everyone in the warehouse and factory must wear either safety shoes or boots with steel toes. There are no exceptions to these rules.

If you said that the main idea is safety rules or safety at work, you are correct. The sentence that does not belong is the one about organizing tools. While this sentence may be true and about work, it is not about safety at work, which is the main idea of the paragraph.

EXERCISE 10

Directions: Read each paragraph below. Cross off the sentences that are not relevant.

1. My kids had a lot of fun last summer. Right after school let out, we went camping for a week. Then they started day camp. They were gone at day camp from 8:30 A.M. until 3:30 P.M. They swam, went on picnics and field trips, and played sports. Then they went to stay with their grandparents in the country for two weeks. They had to work on the farm, but they also got to ride horses and go to the county fair. They had fun before school let out, too, going on a Boy Scout camping trip in May. Finally, just before school started, we went camping again, for a week.

2. My friend Stephen is an amazing guy. He got his GED two years ago. He had been an actor for 10 years before he got his GED, but after he got his GED he decided to go to acting school. He auditioned at schools in New York, Chicago, and Hollywood and got a scholarship to study at Ivan School of Acting in New York City. Soon after he moved there, he got a job in a national TV commercial, and he made a lot of money. Now he has a nice car and good clothes, and is working toward an exciting career in acting. My other best friend, Marty, isn't as lucky as Stephen.

Answers are on page 277.

GED Connection

Directions: Choose the <u>one best answer</u> to each question.

(A)

(1) It's 7:30 A.M. (2) You haven't left the house yet, and you're already late for work. (3) Suddenly you remember that you need to buy a bus pass. (4) You were going to do that last night. (5) You also realize that you have to sign a permission slip for your daughter's field trip on Friday. (6) You should have turned in the permission slip two days ago. (7) What's the matter? (8) You have a common problem—procrastination—which means putting things off into the future. (9) Luckily, there are some ways to avoid procrastination—know your goals, use a datebook, and use to-do lists.

(B)

(10) The first step in avoiding procrastination is knowing your goals. (11) If you know what you want to achieve, it's easier to keep track of what you need to do. (12) For example, your goals might be as simple as doing a good job at work, serving a hot, home-cooked meal to your family five nights a week, and spending every Saturday with your children.

(C)

(13) Knowing your goals will help you decide what tasks you need to focus on in order to achieve your goals.

(D)

(14) Using a datebook also helps. In your datebook you should record all important appointments, such as your work schedule, birthdays, school conferences, and so on. (15) That way, you will not forget any important appointments. (16) You should write each appointment in the date book the same day that you make it and check your datebook at least once a day. (17) That way, you cannot forget anything. (18) Last, create a to-do list each day. (19) Use your datebook to help you do this. (20) Include all errands, appointments, and other things you need to do. (21) Then keep your list with you. (22) That way, it's hard to forget anything. (23) You also need to make sure that you keep a record of all your expenses.

(E)

(24) Everyone procrastinates once in a while, but knowing your goals, using a datebook, and keeping a to-do list will help you stay focused on your goals and the steps you need to follow to achieve them. (25) You will soon notice that your stress level goes down as you begin to meet your goals more efficiently.

1. **Sentence 13: Knowing your goals will help you decide what tasks you need to focus on in order to achieve your goals.**

   Which revision should be made to sentence 13?

   (1) move sentence 13 to the end of paragraph B
   (2) move sentence 13 to the beginning of paragraph D
   (3) move sentence 13 to follow sentence 11
   (4) remove sentence 13
   (5) no revision is necessary

2. **Sentence 18: Last, create a to-do list each day.**

   Which revision should be made to sentence 18 to Improve paragraph D?

   (1) move sentence 18 to follow sentence 14
   (2) move sentence 18 to follow sentence 16
   (3) remove sentence 18
   (4) begin a new paragraph with sentence 18
   (5) no revision is necessary

3. Which revision would make paragraph D more effective?

   (1) move sentence 23 to the beginning of paragraph D
   (2) move sentence 22 to the beginning of paragraph D
   (3) move sentence 22 to the end of paragraph D
   (4) remove sentence 22
   (5) remove sentence 23

Answers are on pages 277–278.

WRITING A GED ESSAY: *The Five-Paragraph Essay*

- A five-paragraph essay is a good way to write a GED essay.

- A five-paragraph essay has an introductory paragraph, three body paragraphs, and a concluding paragraph.

- The introductory paragraph is organized from general to specific and ends with a thesis statement that indicates the contents of the body paragraphs.

- The introductory paragraph should raise the reader's interest in the essay. The writer should tell a personal story, give an interesting statistic, or relate the topic to the reader.

- The body paragraphs each begin with a topic sentence that restates part of the thesis statement. The rest of the sentences give specific facts and details to back up the topic sentence.

- The concluding paragraph is organized from specific to general. It sums up the main ideas of the body paragraphs and relates them to broader issues.

- Each paragraph should contain one main idea. The remaining sentences should support the main idea.

GED Practice

Directions: Use the four steps of the writing process to create a five-paragraph essay that responds to the following GED essay topic. Follow the steps below.

── **T O P I C** ──

What is the nicest experience you have had with your family or friends?

In your essay, describe the nicest experience you have had with your family or friends. Explain why it was so nice. Use your personal observations, experience, and knowledge.

1. Gather Ideas

Read the essay topic and think of the main idea for your five-paragraph essay. Write your main idea on the line below.

Main idea: _____

On the separate sheet of paper, gather ideas using an idea map or brainstorming.

2. Organize Your Ideas

A. Review your idea map or list. Use the following checklist. Add missing information and cross off extra information.

    1. ☐ My idea map or list gives specific details.

    2. ☐ All my supporting ideas back up the main idea.

B. Decide the order in which you will write your essay. Number the ideas in this order.

3. Write Your Essay

Use your idea map or list to write a good five-paragraph essay on a separate sheet of paper. Use the essay diagram on page 164 to help you. Make sure your introductory paragraph is interesting. Tell a personal story, give an interesting statistic, or relate the topic to the reader. Do not spend a lot of time worrying about grammar, punctuation, or spelling. You will check for mistakes after you write your essay.

4. Revise Your Essay

A. Check your essay's ideas and organization using the following list.

    1. ☐ My introductory paragraph is organized from general to specific and ends with a thesis statement.

    2. ☐ My introductory paragraph is interesting.

    3. ☐ My body paragraphs each begin with a topic sentence that accurately sums up what each paragraph is about.

    4. ☐ My concluding paragraph is organized from specific to general.

    5. ☐ My concluding paragraph sums up the main idea of the essay and relates it to broader issues.

B. Check your essay for standards of Edited American English.

    1. ☐ My essay contains no irrelevant ideas.

    2. ☐ Each paragraph in my essay contains only one main idea.

    3. ☐ Each main idea in my essay is discussed in only one body paragraph.

Answers are on page 278.

Writing and Life

Directions: Use the four steps of the writing process to create a five-paragraph essay that responds to the following essay topic. Write your essay on a separate sheet of paper.

—— T O P I C ——

What are some characteristics of a good employee?

In your essay, state some of the characteristics of a good employee. Explain why these characteristics are important. Use your personal observations, experience, and knowledge.

Answers are on page 278.

Self-Assessment

Part A

Directions: Ask your instructor or a friend to review your work on page 175, or review it yourself. Answer the following questions. Write **yes** or **no** on the appropriate line below.

1. _____ Is the introductory paragraph organized from general to specific and does it end with a thesis statement?

2. _____ Is the introductory paragraph interesting?

3. _____ Does each body paragraph begin with a topic sentence that accurately sums up what the paragraph is about?

4. _____ Is the concluding paragraph organized from specific to general?

5. _____ Does the concluding paragraph sum up the main idea of the essay and relate it to broader issues?

6. _____ Does the essay contain any irrelevant ideas?

7. _____ Does each paragraph contain only one main idea?

8. _____ Is each main idea discussed in only one body paragraph?

Part B

Directions: Based on your answers to Part A, respond to the statements below.

1. Name a new strength in your writing that you want to continue to use in future assignments.

   _____

2. Name a feature of your writing that you want to improve by reviewing the information in Chapter 10.

   _____

Answers are on page 278.

CHAPTER 11

Persuasion

A persuasive essay is designed to convince someone to do something. Read the essay topic and persuasive essay below.

————— **T O P I C** —————

Why should people stop smoking?

In your essay, state why people should stop smoking. Give reasons to support your beliefs. Use your personal observations, experience, and knowledge.

Of all bad habits, smoking is one of the worst. It is expensive and harmful to smokers' health. People should stop smoking immediately because it's unattractive, expensive, and dangerous.

Smoking makes people unattractive. People look terrible with a cigarette hanging out of their mouths. In addition, people who smoke often smell of smoke. Since cigarette smoke tends to linger on a smoker's breath, it is often unpleasant to hug or kiss someone who has been smoking.

Cigarette smoking is also expensive. Cigarettes now cost more than $2 a pack in many places. If a person smokes a pack of cigarettes a day, he or she will spend more than $700 per year on cigarettes. In addition, smokers often spend money on lighters, matches, and ashtrays.

Most important, cigarette smoking is terrible for people's health. Smokers are more vulnerable to coughs and colds than nonsmokers. Even worse, smoking causes cancer, emphysema, and heart disease. In fact, smokers on average live seven years less than people who do not smoke. Finally, because cigarette smoking lowers the level of oxygen in the blood, pregnant women who smoke often have babies with low birth weights.

For these reasons, people should stop smoking immediately. People will live happier, wealthier, and healthier lives as a result.

Answer the following questions:

1. What does the writer want to persuade the reader to do?

2. What reasons does the writer give?

3. Does the writer believe that there are any good reasons for people to smoke?

LEARNING TO WRITE: *A Persuasive Essay*

Persuasive writing is used to convince the reader to believe something or to do something. You see persuasive writing all the time. Ads try to persuade you to buy a certain product. Political essays try to persuade you to vote for a certain candidate or to support a certain issue. Articles on health care try to persuade you to follow a low-fat diet, to get more exercise, or to eat more fruits and vegetables. Which of the following sentences is an example of persuasive writing?

Alaska is bigger than Texas.

Live the good life—move to Texas!

If you said that the second sentence is an example of persuasion, you are correct. It is encouraging people to take a certain action—moving to Texas. The first sentence is a statement of fact.

EXERCISE 1

Directions: Which of the following essay topics would require you to use persuasion? Circle the number of the appropriate topics.

1. Should parents limit the amount of TV their children watch?

2. Why did you have a terrible day?

3. Is a new school needed in your neighborhood?

4. What is your favorite kind of pet? Why do you like this kind of pet so much?

5. What are the advantages and disadvantages of traveling by bus?

6. Do people need to get computer training?

7. What is the most interesting place you have ever visited?

8. What is your neighborhood like?

9. Do people need to get more exercise?

10. Why do people need to drive more carefully?

Answers are on page 278.

When you persuade, you need to give reasons. The reasons encourage the reader to follow your advice. For example, if you want to persuade someone that a new parking lot is needed downtown, you might say that people have to spend fifteen or twenty minutes looking for a spot or that people have to park illegally in order to run quick errands. Which of the following sentences would also be a reason to persuade people that a new parking lot is needed?

At busy times, customers go to the mall instead of downtown because they know they can park at the mall.

A new parking lot would destroy the historic homes just east of the downtown shopping area.

If you said that the first sentence would also persuade people to support the new parking lot, you are correct. This sentence gives another reason why more parking is needed—the downtown area is losing customers. The second sentence is a reason to persuade people <u>not</u> to build a new parking lot—the new lot would destroy a historic area.

EXERCISE 2

Directions: Read each topic below and determine which of the two sentences that follows is a specific reason that backs up the topic. Check the appropriate box.

1. A big city is the best place to live.

   a. ☐ My favorite uncle lives in a big city.

   b. ☐ In the city you can find nearly everything you need within a few blocks of your home.

2. People should get plenty of exercise.

   a. ☐ My husband jogs four miles every morning.

   b. ☐ Cardiovascular exercise, such as jogging, will help decrease a person's risk of heart disease.

3. You should spend your next vacation in Florida.

   a. ☐ You can get a really good rate at hotels near Disney World.

   b. ☐ Be sure to pack lots of warm weather clothing.

4. People should not talk on cell phones while driving.

   a. ☐ Some people can receive e-mail messages on their cell phones.

   b. ☐ It is easier to become distracted while talking on a cell phone.

Answers are on page 278.

EXERCISE 3

Directions: Read the following topics. Write a specific reason that backs up
each statement.

1. Our city needs to build a new school building.

   _____

2. People should take public transportation to work.

   _____

3. People should eat plenty of fruits and vegetables.

   _____

4. Parents should make sure their kids wear their seatbelts.

   _____

5. Everyone should recycle.

   _____

Answers are on page 278.

    A persuasive essay should follow the normal organization of a one-, three-,
or five-paragraph essay. A five-paragraph essay, such as the essay on page 178,
should have an introductory paragraph, three body paragraphs, and a
concluding paragraph. The introductory paragraph should have a thesis
statement, and each body paragraph should have a topic sentence.

EXERCISE 4

Directions: Look again at the essay on page 178. Respond to the statements
below.

1. Write *introduction*, *body paragraph 1*, *body paragraph 2*, *body
   paragraph 3*, and *conclusion* next to the appropriate paragraph.

2. Circle the topic sentence in each body paragraph.

3. Underline the thesis statement.

EXPANDING IDEAS: *Outlines*

An **outline** is a good way to help you organize an essay. An outline organizes information into points and subpoints. Look at ideas the writer gathered for the essay on smoking.

cigarettes look terrible

smokers smell of smoke

$2 a pack

over $700 per year

lighters, matches, and ashtrays

coughs and colds

causes cancer, emphysema, and heart disease

smokers have bad breath

smokers live seven years less than nonsmokers

smoking causes problems for unborn babies

Now look at the outline the writer created to organize these ideas.

A. Introduction
  1. There are many bad habits
  2. Smoking is a really bad one
  3. Thesis statement: smoking is unattractive, expensive, and dangerous

B. Unattractive
  1. Cigarettes look terrible
  2. Smokers smell of smoke
  3. Smokers have bad breath

C. Expensive
  1. $2 a pack
  2. Over $700 per year
  3. Lighters, matches, and ashtrays

D. Bad for health
  1. Coughs and colds
  2. Causes cancer, emphysema, and heart disease
  3. Smokers live seven years less than nonsmokers

E. Conclusion—people should quit immediately

Notice the following features of an outline:

- An outline organizes information into groups—one for each of the paragraphs of the essay.

- An outline is written in brief notes and phrases.

- In the completed essay each phrase expands into one or more complete sentences.

- The wording of the completed sentences can be different from the wording in the outline.

- The outline provides brief ideas for the introductory paragraph, the thesis statement, and the conclusion.

- The name of each group expands to become the topic sentence for each body paragraph.

EXERCISE 5

Directions: Look at the following idea list. Use it to complete the outline below.

running burns calories

you can run in parks, along the beach, or in forest preserves

running lowers blood pressure and cholesterol

running gets your mind off your problems

running lets you have some fun

you can see birds, trees, and squirrels

A. Introduction

B. Good for your health

    1. _____

    2. _____

C. Relaxing

    1. _____

    2. _____

D. Contact with nature

    1. _____

    2. _____

E. Conclusion

Answers are on page 278.

EXERCISE 6

Part A

Directions: Look at the following essay topic. Use the space below to create an idea list for an essay on that topic.

——————————— **TOPIC** ———————————

Name a good habit. How can you get someone to adopt that habit?

In your essay, identify a good habit and give reasons to convince people to adopt it. Use your personal observations, experience, and knowledge.

Part B

Directions: Use your idea list to create an outline for your essay in the space below.

Answers are on page 278.

Once your outline is finished, you can write your essay by expanding the words and phrases into complete sentences. Look at the chart below. It compares items from the outline and essay on smoking.

Outline	Essay
Thesis statement: smoking is unattractive, expensive, and dangerous	People should stop smoking immediately because it's unattractive, expensive, and dangerous.
cigarettes look terrible	People look terrible with a cigarette hanging out of their mouths.
over $700 per year	If a person smokes a pack of cigarettes a day, he or she will spend over $700 per year on cigarettes.

Notice that the wording is different—the writer expanded the notes and used them to create longer and more interesting sentences. Also notice that the writer added an additional idea to the essay that was not in the outline. Can you find the sentence in the essay on page 178?

If you chose *Finally, because cigarette smoking lowers the level of oxygen in the blood, pregnant women who smoke often have babies with low birth weights*, you are correct. The writer thought of this idea while writing, and added it to make the essay stronger.

EXERCISE 7

Directions: Look at the outline you created in Exercise 6. Expand the information in the first two sections of the essay into sentences for two paragraphs—the introduction and the first body paragraph. If you think of an additional supporting idea while you are writing, add it to the body paragraph.

_____

_____

_____

_____

_____

_____

Answers are on page 278.

LOOKING AT LANGUAGE: *Sentence Structure and Organization*

Subordinating Conjunctions

A **subordinating conjunction** is used to join a dependent clause to an independent clause in a complex sentence.

> People should stop smoking **because** it is harmful to their health.

> **If** pregnant women smoke, they may cause harm to their unborn children.

Subordinating conjunctions are often used in persuasive writing to show the reasons for something or the consequences of something. Look at the following chart:

Meaning	Subordinating Conjunction	Example
To show reasons	since because so that in order that	People should stop smoking **because** it can cause cancer. **Since** smoking causes cancer, people should quit or cut down. Amanda stopped smoking **so that** her baby would remain healthy.
To show a consequence	if unless whether	**If** people stop smoking now, their lungs will begin to heal. **Unless** you stop smoking, you run the risk of developing heart disease.

EXERCISE 8

Directions: Look again at the essay on page 178. Circle the subordinating conjunctions.

Answers are on page 278.

EXERCISE 9

Directions: Use the subordinating conjunction in parentheses to join each pair of sentences below.

1. People stop smoking now. They will save a lot of money. *(if)*

   _____

2. He started getting more exercise. He needed to lower his blood pressure. *(because)*

   _____

3. Mary Beth joined a gym. She could use the weight machines. *(so that)*

   _____

4. Jayson stopped eating potato chips. They are high in fat. *(since)*

   _____

5. Roberta may get cancer. She stops smoking. *(unless)*

   _____

Answers are on page 278.

Unclear Pronouns

When you write a persuasive essay, you are trying to persuade a person or a group of people to do something. It is very important that your writing remains clear so your audience can follow your thoughts.

In order to make your essay less repetitive, you should use pronouns to refer to your audience. Pronouns should always have a clear **antecedent**. The reader should be able to tell exactly to *whom* or *what* each pronoun refers. Look at the following sentences. Which one has an unclear pronoun?

I found the missing purse and gave it to the woman who lost it.

While Bill was talking to Mr. Maguire, he got angry.

The second sentence has an unclear pronoun. It is not clear whether *he* refers to Bill or Mr. Maguire. In the first sentence, the pronoun it has a clear reference—*purse*.

When a pronoun is unclear, replace it with a noun, or rewrite it in a way that is clearer.

While he was talking to Mr. Maguire, Bill got angry.

Sometimes a pronoun has no clear antecedent, or noun to refer to. Which of the following sentences has a pronoun with no clear antecedent?

We need to fight poverty and injustice in the world so that they have the opportunity to get ahead and succeed in life.

I wrote to my senators and representatives to express my ideas, and they responded to my letters right away.

If you said that the first sentence contains a pronoun with no clear antecedent, you are correct. It is unclear to whom the word *they* refers in this sentence. It could refer to people in third world countries, to unemployed youth in the United States, or to some other group. To fix this problem, replace the pronoun with a more specific noun:

We need to fight poverty and injustice in the world so that people in all countries have the opportunity to get ahead and succeed in life.

EXERCISE 10

Directions: In each sentence below, circle the pronoun that is unclear. Then rewrite the sentence so that the antecedent is clear.

1. Mark spoke to Bill, and then he called Marisa.

_____

2. The city organized music festivals and art fairs so that they would come from all over to visit.

_____

3. Maria doesn't know Ana, but she knows Chen.

_____

4. I bought ice cream cones for my nephews Ricky and Billy, but he didn't eat his.

_____

5. Government officials want to raise their taxes.

_____

Answers are on page 278.

Parallel Structure

Conjunctions such as *and* or *but* are often used to connect a series of elements, such as nouns, verbs, and phrases. Look at the following examples:

> People should stop smoking immediately because it's unattractive, expensive, and dangerous.

> Smokers often spend money on lighters, matches, and ashtrays.

Notice that the connected elements in each sentence are in the same grammatical form—in other words they have **parallel structure**. In the first sentence, the parallel elements are adjectives. In the second sentence, they are nouns.

Look at the following sentence. Does it have parallel structure?

> Sean quit smoking, started exercising, and to begin eating healthfully.

If you said the sentence does not have parallel structure, you are correct. The first two connected elements contain verbs in the past tense—*quit* and *started*, while the third element contains an infinitive—*to begin*. Now read the sentence rewritten in parallel structure:

> Sean quit smoking, started exercising, and began eating healthfully.

Using parallel structure when you write a persuasive essay will help to keep your writing strong and your argument convincing.

EXERCISE 11

Directions: Rewrite each sentence below in parallel structure.

1. He stopped smoking and to eat fatty foods.

   _____

2. Mrs. Barnes is nervous, insecure, and disrespectfully.

   _____

3. The waitress took our order, brought us our drinks, but forgets to bring us our sandwiches.

   _____

4. My favorite hobbies are running, going to the movies, and to read.

   _____

Answers are on page 278.

GED Connection

Directions: Choose the <u>one best answer</u> to each question.

Employee Fitness Program

(A)

(1) In order to promote a healthier workforce, Eastern Services Corporation has started a new Wellness Program. (2) This program is designed to help employees get more exercise, cutting down on unhealthful habits, and develop healthful habits. (3) Listed below are just some of the new programs and benefits.

(B)

(3) We will offer special Stop Smoking classes during work hours for employees who smoke. (4) The employees cut down on cigarettes or stop smoking entirely. (5) The classes will be free and offered before and after work and during lunch breaks.

(C)

(6) We have arranged for special discounted memberships at Global Gym so that they can get memberships at special prices. (7) Global Gyms has locations all over the metro area. (8) Employees can get memberships for only $99, plus a monthly fee of $7.95. (9) The gyms have weight rooms, indoor tracks, lap pools, and there are also basketball courts.

(D)

(10) All employees will get special discounts on health and life insurance. (11) Everyone will be receiving insurance forms in order to request the discount.

(E)

(12) We will be making further announcements about additional programs and services in the Wellness Program. (13) We will also be starting a Wellness Committee to help direct the program. (14) If you are interested in serving on this committee, please get an application form from Human Resources.

1. **Sentence 2: This program is designed to help employees get more exercise, <u>cutting down on unhealthful habits</u>, and develop healthful habits.**

   Which is the best way to write the underlined portion of the text? If the original is the best way, choose option (1).

   (1) cutting down on unhealthful habits
   (2) help cutting down on unhealthful habits
   (3) and cutting down on unhealthful habits
   (4) cut down on unhealthful habits
   (5) employees cut down on unhealthful habits

2. **Sentences 3 and 4: We will offer special Stop Smoking classes during work hours for employees who smoke. The employees cut down on cigarettes or stop smoking entirely.**

   The most effective combination of sentences 3 and 4 would include which group of words?

   (1) smoke, but the employees
   (2) smoke so that the employees
   (3) smoke because the employees
   (4) smoke, the employees
   (5) smoke the employees

3. **Sentence 6: We have arranged for special discounted memberships at Global Gym so that they can get memberships at special prices.**

   What correction should be made to sentence 6?

   (1) replace *they* with *employees*
   (2) replace *they* with *he or she*
   (3) replace *so that* with *although*
   (4) replace *they* with *them*
   (5) no correction is necessary

4. **Sentence 9: The gyms have weight rooms, indoor tracks, lap pools, <u>and there are also basketball courts</u>.**

   Which is the best way to write the underlined portion of the text? If the original is the best way, choose option (1).

   (1) and there are also basketball courts
   (2) and playing basketball
   (3) but there are also basketball courts
   (4) and they have basketball courts
   (5) and basketball courts

WRITING A GED ESSAY: *Persuasion*

- Persuasive writing attempts to convince the reader to do something or to believe something.

- Persuasive writing provides plenty of reasons for the reader to accept the writer's ideas.

- An outline is a good way to organize information for a persuasive essay.

- An outline is written in words and phrases. The words and phrases expand to sentences in the completed essay.

- Subordinating conjunctions such as *since, because, if,* and *unless* should be used to show reasons and consequences.

- All pronouns should clearly refer to another noun in the sentence or paragraph.

- Parallel structure should be used when joining items in a series.

GED Practice

Directions: Use the four steps of the writing process to create a five-paragraph persuasive essay that responds to the following GED essay topic. Follow the steps below.

——————————— T O P I C ———————————

Why should people get more exercise?

In your essay state why people should get more exercise. Give reasons to support your beliefs. Use your personal observations, experience, and knowledge.

1. **Gather Ideas**

   Read the essay topic and think of the main idea for your five-paragraph essay. Write your main idea on the line below.

   Main idea: _____

   Brainstorm an idea list on a separate sheet of paper.

2. Organize Your Ideas

Create an outline to organize the ideas in your idea list. Then check your outline using the following checklist. Add missing information and cross off extra information.

1. ☐ My outline contains specific details.

2. ☐ All the ideas support my thesis statement.

3. Write Your Essay

Use your outline to write a good five-paragraph essay on a separate sheet of paper. Do not spend a lot of time worrying about grammar, punctuation, or spelling. You will check for mistakes after you write your essay.

4. Revise Your Essay

A. Check your essay's ideas and organization using the following list.

1. ☐ My essay contains plenty of reasons to persuade the reader.

2. ☐ Each paragraph in my essay is about one main idea.

3. ☐ My thesis statement lists the main idea of each body paragraph.

B. Check your essay for standards of Edited American English.

1. ☐ I used subordinating conjunctions to join dependent and independent clauses.

2. ☐ My pronoun references are clear.

3. ☐ My writing uses parallel structure.

Answers are on page 279.

Writing and Life

Directions: Use the four steps of the writing process you to create a five-paragraph essay that responds to the following essay topic. Write your essay on a separate sheet of paper.

--- T O P I C ---

What can people do to have a more healthful diet?

In your essay, state what people can do to have a more healthful diet. Give reasons to support your views. Use your personal observations, experience, and knowledge.

Answers are on page 279.

Self-Assessment

Part A

Directions: Ask your instructor or a friend to review your work on page 195, or review it yourself. Answer the following questions. Write **yes** or **no** on the appropriate line below.

1. _____ Does the essay contain plenty of reasons to persuade the reader?

2. _____ Is each paragraph about one main idea?

3. _____ Does the thesis statement list the main idea of each body paragraph?

4. _____ Are subordinating conjunctions used to join dependent and independent clauses?

5. _____ Are all pronoun references clear?

6. _____ Are sentences written in parallel structure?

Part B

Directions: Based on your answers to Part A, respond to the statements below.

1. Name a new strength in your writing that you want to continue to use in future assignments.

   _____

2. Name a feature of your writing that you want to improve by reviewing the information in Chapter 11.

   _____

Answers are on page 279.

CHAPTER 12

Improving Your Writing

In this book you learned many different ways to write a good GED essay. In each style of writing and in each type of essay, you have used a four-step writing process. One of the most important steps of this process is evaluating your work—making sure your essay is the best it can be. When you revise, you check your completed essay for organization, relevance, Edited American English, and word choice. In this chapter you will learn several ways to further improve your writing in terms of the criteria in the GED Essay Scoring Guide.

Look at the following topic and essay. How can the essay be improved?

--- T O P I C ---

Why is the cost of raising children going up every year?

In your essay, explain why the cost of raising children is going up every year. Use your personal observations, experience, and knowledge.

I really worry about my family. It's so hard to raise kids these days. One of the biggest worries is the rising cost of living. There are three main areas where rising costs worry parents: food, clothing, and shelter.

The cost of food keeps going up. For example, last year milk cost $1.99 a gallon. This year it went up to $2.39, and that's too much.

The cost of clothing also keeps rising. Last year, I had spent only about $150 on school clothes for my kids. This fall, that went up to $200.

Third, the cost of shelter keeps going up, too. My rent went up $40 this year, and one of my kids needs a new bed—that's also espensive. Of course, that bed will need new sheets and pillowcases, and also cost money. In addition, the cost for laundering all of these clothes and linens has gone up, too. The Laundromat on my block used to charge fify cents for a wash or a dry. Those went up to a dollar last week. I do at least five loads of laundry a week, so that really adds up.

Answer the following questions:

1. Does the essay address the topic?

2. Is the essay organized?

3. Does the essay contain plenty of details and supporting examples?

4. Is the essay written in Edited American English (EAE)?

5. Does the essay have varied word choice or is the vocabulary repetitive?

Understanding the GED Essay Scoring Guide

The GED Essay Scoring Guide focuses on five areas:

- Response to the prompt
- Organization
- Development and details
- Conventions of Edited American English
- Word choice

Response to the Prompt

This area focuses on whether your essay answers the GED essay topic. For example, if the topic asks you to explain why you believe that taxes need to be lowered, your essay needs to focus on this issue only. In order to receive a high score, your essay needs to provide plenty of information that is about the topic and avoid information that is off-topic. Look at the following paragraphs. Which one is about the topic of the need to reduce taxes?

> Taxes are simply too high for working families. Families have to pay both state and federal income taxes. In some cities families have to pay a city income tax, too. Even worse, many families pay special taxes on their telephone bills, gas, plane tickets, and other purchases. A recent study estimated that families take the first four months of the year just to make enough to pay their taxes.

> Nowadays, expenses keep increasing for families. Families have to pay rising costs for basics such as food and shelter. Taxes also seem to keep rising each year. The cost of clothing, another basic need that no one can do without, keeps going up too. Insurance, too, keeps becoming more and more expensive.

If you said that the first paragraph addresses the essay topic of the need to lower taxes, you are correct. The second focuses on a much broader topic—the rising cost of living for all families.

Organization

This area focuses on whether your essay is organized. Your essay needs to have an overall pattern or organization, such as description, narration, cause and effect, comparison/contrast, and so on. Then it needs to follow that pattern throughout the entire essay. This includes having clear introductory, body, and concluding paragraphs.

Read the following paragraph. What is the problem with its organization?

> My kids had a lot of fun yesterday during our visit to Chicago. First, we went to the aquarium, which is a museum dedicated to marine life. We saw hundreds of fish. After that, we went to a mall. We bought some souvenirs and then rode on a huge Ferris wheel. After that, we went to an art museum. It was having a special exhibition on Latino artists. Then we drove back to our home in southern Illinois. Earlier in the morning we also had a great breakfast at a pancake restaurant. Our day was a lot of fun.

If you said that the paragraph has problems with chronological order, you are correct. The essay is in chronological order except for the information about breakfast at the pancake house, which is placed at the end of the essay.

Development and Details

Development and details refer to the support for your ideas. Good writers always back up their ideas with plenty of examples and support. Suppose you are writing about reasons that the cost of living is increasing. If all you do is mention prices of one kind of item, such as food, you will not have much support for your ideas. You need to mention other examples, such as shelter and clothing, too. Read the following paragraphs. Which one contains more support for its main idea?

> I think that the government needs to do something about the rising cost of living. Last year, my rent went up 20 percent! In addition, food and clothing also got much more expensive. My weekly supermarket bill went from $80 to $100. Also, the cost of riding the bus went up 25 cents—a real hardship for people who ride the bus to work or school every day.

> I think that the government needs to do something about the rising cost of living. My rent went up $40 last month, and that's for a tiny apartment in an old building. I have only a bedroom and a kitchen. There is no living room and the bathroom is very small. In addition, electric rates went up last month, too, so now staying at home and watching TV just got more expensive, too.

The first paragraph contains plenty of support for why the government needs to do something about the cost of living. The second paragraph is much more focused on just the cost of housing—rent and electricity. The writer needs to include information on other costs in order to make his essay convincing.

Conventions of Edited American English

The conventions of Edited American English include such things as sentence structure, verb agreement, and so on. Look at the following sentences. Which one follows the conventions of Edited American English?

The cost of gas and electricity has went up, to.

My gas and electric bills went up 20 percent this year.

The second sentence follows the conventions of Edited American English. The subject and verb agree, the words are spelled correctly, and the sentence contains proper capitalization and end punctuation.

The first sentence contains errors in subject-verb agreement and in spelling. Here is the corrected sentence:

The cost of gas and electricity **have gone** up, **too.**

Word Choice

When you write, you should vary your word choice to provide variety and interest for the reader. Look at the following sentences. Which one has better word choice?

We went to the movies last night and saw a really funny movie.

We went to the Century Theater last night and saw a hilarious movie about bumbling cops and robbers.

If you said that the second sentence has better word choice, you are correct. It used specific words such as *Century Theater, hilarious,* and *bumbling.* The first sentence repeats the word *movie* and uses the weak description *really funny.*

EXERCISE 1

Directions: Match the evaluation criteria with their definitions. Write the appropriate letter on each line.

1. _____ Response to the prompt

2. _____ Organization

3. _____ Development and details

4. _____ Conventions of Edited American English

5. _____ Word choice

a. essay follows a pattern and has introductory, body, and concluding paragraphs

b. essay contains plenty of specific information to back up the main idea

c. essay addresses the topic

d. vocabulary is varied and rich

e. essay is grammatically correct

Answers are on page 279.

Reviewing the GED Essay Scoring Guide

Look again at the copy of the actual GED Essay Scoring Guide on the next page. Notice that the four-point scoring scale appears in the first row of the chart and the five criteria are listed in the first column. The rest of the chart contains descriptions of each criterion for writing with a score of 1 *(inadequate)* to 4 *(effective)*. Take some time review the five criteria and scores, and then complete the exercise below.

EXERCISE 2

Part A

Directions: Review the essay on page 198. Then rate it using the GED Essay Scoring Guide on the next page. Choose a number for each of the rating criteria. Then give the essay an overall score.

Part B

Directions: Which areas of the GED scoring criteria should the writer focus on improving? Check the appropriate boxes.

☐ Response to the prompt

☐ Organization

☐ Development and details

☐ Conventions of Edited American English

☐ Word choice

Answers are on page 279.

Language Arts, Writing, Part II
Essay Scoring Guide

	1 Inadequate	2 Marginal	3 Adequate	4 Effective
	Reader has difficulty identifying or following the writer's ideas.	**Reader occasionally has difficulty understanding or following the writer's ideas.**	**Reader understands the writer's ideas.**	**Reader understands and easily follows the writer's expression of ideas.**
Response to the Prompt	Attempts to address the prompt but with little or no success in establishing a focus.	Addresses the prompt, though the focus may shift.	Uses the prompt to establish a main idea.	Presents a clearly focused main idea that addresses the prompt.
Organization	Fails to organize ideas.	Shows some evidence of an organizational plan.	Uses an identifiable organizational plan.	Establishes a clear and logical organization.
Development and Details	Demonstrates little or no development; usually lacks details or examples or presents irrelevant information.	Has some development but lacks specific details; may be limited to a listing, repetitions, or generalizations.	Has focused but occasionally uneven development; incorporates some specific detail.	Achieves coherent development with specific and relevant details and examples.
Conventions of EAE	Exhibits minimal or no control of sentence structure and the conventions of Edited American English (EAE).	Demonstrates inconsistent control of sentence structure and the conventions of EAE.	Generally controls sentence structure and the conventions of EAE.	Consistently controls sentence structure and the conventions of EAE.
Word Choice	Exhibits weak and/or inappropriate words.	Exhibits a narrow range of word choice, often including inappropriate selections.	Exhibits appropriate word choice.	Exhibits varied and precise word choice.

EXERCISE 3

Part A

Directions: Read the following actual GED essay topic and essay below. Then rate the essay using the GED Essay Scoring Guide on page 203. Choose a number for each of the rating criteria. Then give the essay an overall score.

————————————— T O P I C —————————————

If you could make one positive change to your daily life, what would that change be?

In your essay, identify the change you would make. Explain the reasons for your choice. Use your personal observations, experience, and knowledge.

——

> If I could make one positive change in my life the change would be in my attitude. I would change my attitude toward certain people I think is outrageous, these certain people are those people who think they're better than everybody else and I would also change my attitude toward people who are of my age but, act so child like. I would change my attitude toward these people because in the future I may need some of these people that I've treated so negatively. If I continued to treat these people badly I may not amount to anything in the future. My attitude toward life would also have to change I think because I'm doing so well at this point in my life. Life I think is just a game that everyone has to play in order to survive. I'm not playing to survive I playing only to get by. I feel if my attitude doesn't change at this point I will never be able to survive the game. The above things about my attitude have to be my positive change in my daily life.

Reprinted with permission of the GED Testing Service.

Part B

Directions: Which areas of the GED scoring criteria should the writer focus on improving? Check the appropriate boxes.

☐ Response to the prompt

☐ Organization

☐ Development and details

☐ Conventions of Edited American English

☐ Word choice

Answers are on page 279.

Revising Your Essay

Once you have figured out the areas in which you need improvement, you can develop strategies to strengthen your writing. Here are some ideas to help you.

Response to the Prompt

If you are having trouble making sure that the essay is addressing the prompt, try the following techniques:

- Read the essay topic more thoroughly to make sure you understand it. Circle key words such as *why, when, where,* and so on. Look at the following topic. What key words would you circle? How would you respond?

—————————————————— **T O P I C** ——————————————————

The cost of living seems to be increasing every day.

Write an essay explaining why the cost of living is increasing.

The key word you circled was probably why. In your essay you would most likely give examples of why the cost of living is increasing, such as the cost of food, clothing, and shelter.

- When you organize your ideas, reread the essay topic. Make sure that all of the ideas are about the essay topic, and that your ideas address all aspects of the topic. Add or cross off ideas until you have enough relevant support.

Organization

To improve your essay's organization, try the following suggestions:

- Make sure you have chosen the correct pattern of organization: description, narration, comparison/contrast, cause and effect, persuasion, and so on. Look again at the essay topic above. What pattern of organization would you use in your response?

    If you said, cause and effect, you are correct. This essay would most likely be answered by listing causes for the rising cost of living.

- Make sure your essay has an introductory paragraph with a thesis statement, body paragraphs with topic sentences, and a concluding paragraph that summarizes the main ideas of the essay.

Development and Details

Use the following techniques to improve the development and details of your writing:

- Use one of the tools for gathering ideas listed in this book, such as an idea list, a T-chart, or a Venn diagram.

- Use your life experience and reflections as a basis for your ideas.

- Let the ideas you gather suggest more ideas. As you write down ideas, reflect on other ideas you can add to your essay.

Conventions of Edited American English

If you need to improve your Edited American English, consider using one of the following techniques:

- Allow more time for revising when you write.

- Review the sections labeled "Looking at Language" in Chapters 3–11 of this book.

Word Choice

To improve your word choice you can use the following techniques:

- Try to include specific vocabulary when you write.

- Allow more time for revising to check for word choice.

EXERCISE 4

Directions: Look again at the score you gave to the essay in Exercise 3. What suggestions can you give the writer to improve his or her writing? Check the appropriate boxes for each critera below.

1. Response to the Prompt

☐ Read the essay topic more thoroughly to make sure you understand it. Circle key words such as *why, when, where,* and so on.

☐ When you organize your ideas, reread the essay topic. Make sure that all of the ideas are about the essay topic, and that your ideas address all aspects of the topic. Add or cross off ideas until you have enough relevant support.

2. Organization

☐ Make sure you have chosen the correct pattern of organization: description, narration, comparison/contrast, cause and effect, persuasion, and so on.

☐ Make sure your essay has an introductory paragraph with a thesis statement, body paragraphs with topic sentences, and a concluding paragraph that summarizes the main ideas of the essay.

3. Development and Details

☐ Use one of the tools for gathering ideas listed in this book, such as an idea list, a T-chart, or a Venn diagram.

☐ Use your life experience and reflections as a basis for your ideas.

☐ Let the ideas you gather suggest more ideas. As you write ideas, reflect on other ideas you can add to your essay.

4. Edited American English

☐ Allow more time for revising when you write.

☐ Review the sections labeled "Looking at Language" in this book.

5. Word Choice

☐ Try to include specific vocabulary when you write.

☐ Allow more time for revising to check for word choice.

Answers are on page 279.

Making Choices

To improve your chances of scoring well in Part II of the GED Language Arts, Writing Test, you need to focus on the areas that are most important to getting a high score. You also need to focus on improving just one or two aspects of your writing at a time.

The most important areas for getting a good score on the GED essay are response to the prompt, organization, and development and details. If you do well in these areas, your score will not suffer much if you have some problems with Edited American English or word choice.

EXERCISE 5

Directions: Review the boxes you checked in Exercise 4. Keeping the most important areas for getting a high score in mind, write the three areas in which the writer should concentrate on improving.

1. _____

2. _____

3. _____

Answers are on page 279.

WRITING A GED ESSAY: *Improving Your Work*

- In order to improve your writing, you need to focus on the criteria in the GED Essay Scoring Guide.

- The GED Essay Scoring Guide addresses response to the prompt, organization, development and detail, conventions of Edited American English, and word choice.

- The most important areas for obtaining a high score are response to the prompt, organization, and development and detail.

- You should use the scoring criteria to focus on improving your writing in the areas that are most important to success on the GED essay.

GED Practice

Part A

Directions: Use the four steps of the writing process to write an essay that responds to the following GED essay topic. Follow the steps below.

—————— T O P I C ——————

The cost of living seems to be increasing every day.

Write an essay explaining why the cost of living is increasing.

1. **Gather Ideas**

   Read the essay topic and think of the main idea for your essay. Write your main idea on the line below. Then, on a separate sheet of paper, gather ideas for your essay using one of the methods you learned in this book.

   Main idea: _____

2. **Organize Your Ideas**

   Organize the ideas you gathered using one of the methods you learned in this book. Make sure that all the ideas are relevant. Cross off any ideas that are not relevant.

3. **Write Your Essay**

   Use your organized ideas to write a good essay on a separate sheet of paper. Do not spend a lot of time worrying about grammar, punctuation, or spelling. You will check for mistakes after you write your essay

4. **Revise Your Essay**

   Check the information, the organization, and the language you used for grammar and spelling.

Part B

Directions: Rate your essay according to the criteria in the GED Essay Scoring Guide on page 203. Choose a number for each criterion. Then give the essay an overall score. Look at the areas in which you scored well and in which you need to improve. Check the boxes of the following techniques that will help you improve your writing.

1. Response to the Prompt

   ☐ Read the essay topic more thoroughly to make sure you understand it. Circle key words such as *why, when, where,* and so on.

   ☐ When you organize your ideas, reread the essay topic. Make sure that all of the ideas are about the essay topic, and that your ideas address all aspects of the topic. Add or cross off ideas until you have enough relevant support.

2. Organization

   ☐ Make sure you have chosen the correct pattern of organization: description, narration, comparison/contrast, cause and effect, persuasion, and so on.

   ☐ Make sure your essay has an introductory paragraph with a thesis statement, body paragraphs with topic sentences, and a concluding paragraph that summarizes the main ideas of the essay.

3. Development and Details

   ☐ Use one of the tools for gathering ideas listed in this book, such as an idea list, a T-chart, or a Venn diagram.

   ☐ Use your life experience and reflections as a basis for your ideas.

   ☐ Let the ideas you gather suggest more ideas. As you write down ideas, reflect on other ideas you can add to your essay.

4. Edited American English

   ☐ Allow more time for revising when you write.

   ☐ Review the sections labeled "Looking at Language" in this book.

5. Word Choice

   ☐ Try to include specific vocabulary when you write.

   ☐ Allow more time for revising to check for word choice.

Part C

Directions: The most important criteria in the GED Essay Scoring Guide are response to the prompt, organization, and development and detail. Look at the boxes you checked in Part B. On the lines below, write the areas on which you should concentrate to improve your score on the GED essay.

1. _____

2. _____

Answers are on page 279.

Writing and Life

Directions: Use the four steps of the writing process to write an essay that responds to the following essay topic. When revising, pay attention to the areas in which you want to improve your writing. Write your essay on a separate sheet of paper.

TOPIC

What can people do spend their money more wisely?

In your essay, state what people can do to spend their money more wisely. Explain the reasons behind your ideas. Use your personal observations, experience, and knowledge.

Answers are on page 279.

Self-Assessment

Directions: Ask your instructor or a friend to score your essays using the GED Essay Scoring Guide on page 203. Respond to the statements below based on the score you received.

1. Did focusing on your three areas of improvement help you improve your work on this essay? How?

   _____

2. Name a new strength in your writing that you want to continue to use in future assignments.

   _____

3. Name a feature of your writing that you want to continue to improve by reviewing the information in Chapter 12.

   _____

Answers are on page 279.

CHAPTER 13

Review

In this book you have learned a number of techniques and skills to help you write a good GED essay. This chapter provides a review of the techniques and skills in the following table.

Essay Structures		
One-Paragraph	**Three-Paragraph**	**Five-Paragraph**
<ul><li>Topic sentence</li><li>Supporting sentences</li><li>Concluding sentence</li></ul>	<ul><li>Introductory paragraph with thesis statement</li><li>Body paragraph with topic sentence</li><li>Concluding paragraph</li></ul>	<ul><li>Introductory paragraph with thesis statement</li><li>3 body paragraphs with topic sentences</li><li>Concluding paragraph</li><li>Styles of Writing</li></ul>

Styles of Writing	The Writing Process
<ul><li>Description</li><li>Process</li><li>Narration</li><li>Comparison and contrast</li><li>Cause and effect</li><li>Persuasion</li></ul>	<ul><li>Gathering ideas</li><li>Organizing ideas</li><li>Writing</li><li>Revising</li></ul>

Essay Structures

In Chapters 3, 6, and 10 in this book, you learned three different essay structures—the one-, the three-, and the five-paragraph essays.

- The **one-paragraph essay** is the simplest form of essay. It has a very specific structure:

  1. A topic sentence that introduces the main idea of the one paragraph essay.

  2. A number of supporting sentences that back up the topic sentence

  3. A concluding sentence that sums up the main idea of the paragraph and brings the paragraph to a close.

- The **three-paragraph essay** has a slightly more complex structure:

  1. An introductory paragraph that gives a general sense of the main idea

  2. A body paragraph that contains a number of specific supporting sentences that back up the main idea

  3. A concluding paragraph that sums up the main idea and brings the essay to a close

- The **five-paragraph essay** has the most complex structure. This type of essay is the best choice to use for your GED essay. A five-paragraph essay has these parts:

  1. An introductory paragraph that gives a general sense of the main idea

  2. Three body paragraphs that each contain a main idea with supporting sentences to back up each main idea

  3. A concluding paragraph that sums up the main idea and brings the essay to a close

EXERCISE 1

Directions: Which type of essay structure is each phrase about—the one-paragraph, three-paragraph, or five-paragraph essay? Write the name of the appropriate structure on each line. There may be more than one structure for each phrase.

1. _____ one or more topic sentences

2. _____ a thesis statement

3. _____ supporting sentences

4. _____ a concluding paragraph

5. _____ an introductory paragraph

6. _____ three body paragraphs

Answers are on page 279.

EXERCISE 2

Directions: The following paragraphs of a five-paragraph essay are in the wrong order. Number them in order from **1** to **5**.

a. _____ Now you are ready to start cooking. Put the vegetables in a large pot. Rinse the split peas, and add them to the pot, too. Fill the pot with water and put it on the stove. Let it cook for about two hours.

b. _____ In the winter I like to fix hearty soups and stews for my family. They're not very expensive, but they are warm and satisfying. One of everyone's favorites is split pea soup. Making split pea soup is easy if you follow the directions.

c. _____ First, you need to get ready. Gather all of the ingredients. You will need celery, carrots, onions, and a bag of split peas. Cut up the celery, carrots, and onions.

d. _____ When everything is ready, your family will have a nice, hot meal that's easy to fix and not very expensive. Try making split pea soup for supper on Fridays. It's a great meal for the end of the week.

e. _____ When the soup is almost ready, fix something to go with it. My family loves cornbread, so I usually make that. You can also make a large salad or get some French bread from the supermarket.

Answers are on page 279.

Types of Writing

In Chapters 4, 5, 7, 8, 9, and 11 in this book, you learned six styles of writing—description, process, narration, comparison and contrast, cause and effect, and persuasion.

- **Descriptive writing** tells readers what a person, place, or thing is like.

  The chocolate chip cookies were rich, chewy, and delicious.

- **Process writing** tells the reader how to do something.

  To prepare this pizza, cook it for 12 minutes in an oven preheated to 350 degrees.

- **Narrative writing** allows you to write about something that happened in the past.

  I changed the truck's oil, and then I checked the brakes and transmission.

- **Comparative writing** allows you to find similarities between two things. **Contrastive writing** allows you to find differences between two things.

  Alaska is bigger than Texas, but both have petroleum reserves.

- **Cause-and-effect writing** tells the reasons why something happens or happened or tells the results of an event.

  Because of increasing taxes, families have less money to spend on food.

- **Persuasive writing** is used to convince the reader to believe something or to do something.

  Increasing the amount of fiber in your diet is a good way to reduce the risk of heart disease and certain kinds of cancer.

EXERCISE 3

Directions: Read each sentence below. On each line, write the name of the type of writing that best describes each sentence.

1. _____ The old, dilapidated truck was parked at a crazy angle in front of the convenience store.

2. _____ To change the vacuum cleaner bag, open the compartment, remove the old bag, replace it with a new one, and close the compartment.

3. _____ There was a bad rainstorm, so the ball game was canceled.

4. _____ High winds from the storm tore off several roofs and damaged numerous trees and power lines.

5. _____ This year's apple crop was much bigger than last year's.

6. _____ You should exercise more often.

Answers are on page 279.

Getting Ready to Write

When you are preparing to write a GED essay, the first thing you should decide is how to address the topic—with description, process, cause and effect, and so on. Read the following topics. How would you address them?

What is your favorite flavor of ice cream? What does it taste like?

Why should people get more exercise?

If you said that the first topic calls for description and the second for persuasion, you are correct. The first essay topic requires you to describe the flavor of ice cream you like best. The second asks you to persuade readers that people need to get more exercise.

EXERCISE 4

Directions: What type of writing does each essay topic call for? Write the appropriate letter on each line below.

1. _____ Which is better— watching TV or renting a video?

2. _____ How did you spend your last day off?

3. _____ Why do so many people avoid going to the dentist?

4. _____ Why should people go to the dentist more often?

5. _____ What is the nicest present you ever received?

6. _____ How do you make a jack-o'-lantern?

a. Description

b. Process

c. Narration

d. Comparison and contrast

e. Cause and effect

f. Persuasion

Answers are on page 279.

The Writing Process

When you write a GED essay, you have only 45 minutes to write. Therefore, you need an organized plan to allow you to gather enough ideas and to write about them. The writing process is useful because it helps you break your work into four logical steps that take you from ideas to a completed essay. Throughout this book you learned specific techniques to help you with the writing process.

Gathering Ideas

When you **gather ideas**, you examine the topic and think of ideas for your essay. In this book you learned the following techniques for gathering ideas:

- When you create an **idea list**, you simply jot down your ideas in the order in which you think of them.

<u>*My favorite activity—going out with my husband*</u>

we're always busy with work and kids—need time together

laugh, talk

go out together

see a movie

go out to dinner

visit another couple

have dinner with another couple

sometimes we both have to work on Saturdays, so my mother has to baby-sit

go shopping

have fun

mother baby-sits

afterwards, we feel ready to deal with work and kids again

- When you use an **idea map**, you write the ideas in a web-like that shows how the ideas are related.

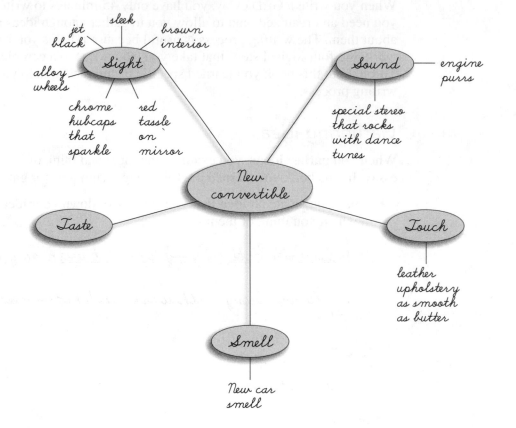

- The ideas in a **flow chart** are put in the order in which they need to occur. A flow chart is useful for gathering ideas for a process essay.

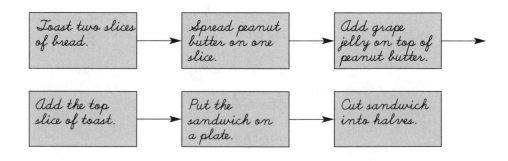

- When you use a **Venn diagram**, you use overlapping circles to show how two things are the same and/or different. Like items are grouped in a common area at the center of the diagram. Different items are grouped separately. A Venn diagram is a good technique when writing a comparison and contrast essay.

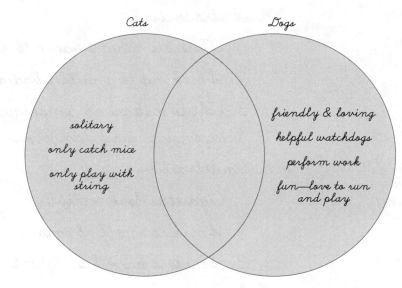

Organizing

When you **organize** your ideas, you arrange them into groups—one for each of the body paragraphs in your essay—and put the groups in the order in which you will deal with them in your essay. You also make sure that the ideas are all about the main idea of the essay.

If you use an idea map to gather ideas, your ideas will already be organized. You just need to number the groups in the order in which you want to write about them in your finished essay.

If you use a different technique to gather ideas, you can use circling and numbering to organize your ideas. Look at the organized Venn diagram below:

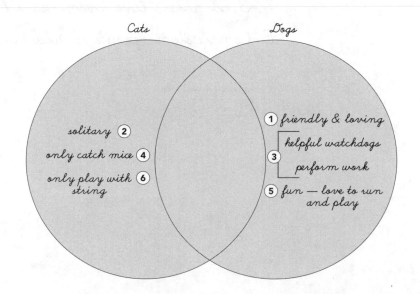

- Another good way to organize your ideas is with an outline. An outline is the most careful way to organize your ideas, but it also takes the most time.

A. Introduction
   1. There are many bad habits
   2. Smoking is a really bad one
   3. Thesis statement: smoking is unattractive, expensive, and dangerous

B. Unattractive
   1. Cigarettes look terrible
   2. Smokers smell of smoke
   3. Smokers have bad breath

C. Expensive
   1. $2 a pack
   2. Over $700 per year
   3. Lighters, matches, and ashtrays

D. Bad for health
   1. Coughs and colds
   2. Causes cancer, emphysema, and heart disease
   3. Smokers live seven years less than nonsmokers

E. Conclusion—people should quit immediately

EXERCISE 5

Directions: Look at the following flow chart. Use circling to put the ideas in three logical groups and name them. Above each circle, write the name of the group.

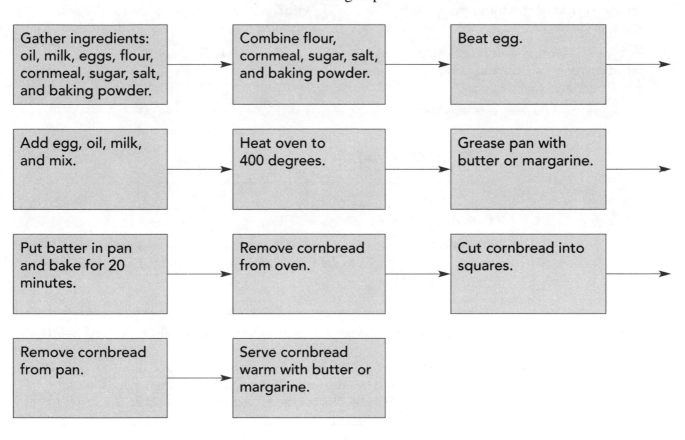

Answers are on page 279.

Writing

In this stage you simply write your essay. When you write, do not worry too much about spelling, grammar, and so on. Just try to write your ideas in complete sentences and paragraphs. You will check the spelling, grammar, and vocabulary in the last step of the writing process.

Revising

When you **revise**, you check your essay with regard to the following areas:

- All your ideas are about the main idea of the essay.

- The essay follows your organizational plan.

- The essay follows the structure of a one-, three-, or five-paragraph essay.

- Your essay is written in complete sentences and does not contain errors in Edited American English.

By following the four steps of the writing process, you will be able to write a strong GED essay in 45 minutes.

WRITING A GED ESSAY: *Review*

In this book you learned the following writing skills and techniques:

- Three different essay structures—the one-paragraph essay, the three-paragraph essay, and the five-paragraph essay

- Six types of writing—description, process, narration, comparison and contrast, cause and effect, and persuasion

- A useful four-step process to follow when writing a GED essay—gathering ideas, organizing ideas, writing, and revising

GED Practice

Part A

Directions: Use the four steps of the writing process to write an essay that responds to the following GED essay topic. Follow the steps below.

———— T O P I C ————

What one improvement does your block or neighborhood need?

In your essay, state the improvement your block or neighborhood needs. Explain the reasons behind your views. Use your personal observations, experience, and knowledge.

1. Gather Ideas

Read the essay topic, decide how you will respond to the question, and think of the main idea for your essay. Write the type of writing and your main idea on the lines below. Then, on a separate sheet of paper, gather ideas using one of the techniques on pages 219–221.

Type of writing: _____

Main idea: _____

2. Organize Your Ideas

Organize the ideas you gathered using one of the techniques on pages 221–222. Make sure that all the ideas are relevant. Cross off any ideas that are not relevant.

3. **Write Your Essay**

   Use your organized ideas to write a good essay on a separate sheet of paper. Do not spend a lot of time worrying about grammar, punctuation, or spelling. You will check for mistakes after you write your essay.

4. **Revise Your Essay**

   Check the information, the organization, and the language you used for grammar and spelling.

Answers are on page 280.

Writing and Life

Directions: Use the four steps of the writing process to write an essay that responds to the following essay topic. Write your essay on a separate sheet of paper.

―――――― T O P I C ――――――

What is the biggest problem our society faces today?

In your essay, state what you believe to be the biggest problem our society faces today. Give reasons to back up your beliefs. Use your personal observations, experience, and knowledge.

Answers are on page 280.

Self-Assessment

Directions: Ask your instructor or a friend to score your essays using the GED Essay Scoring Guide on the inside front cover of this book. Respond to the statements below based on the score you received.

1. Name a new strength in your writing that you want to continue to use in future assignments.

   _____

2. Name a feature of your writing that you want to continue to improve by reviewing the information in Chapter 13.

   _____

   Answers are on page 280.

CHAPTER 14

Taking the Test

You are almost ready for the Language Arts, Writing Test. What do you do to prepare yourself in the last few days before the test? Read the following letter.

March 13

Dear Linda and Jennifer,

Well, I did it! I passed the essay portion of the GED Test! It took some work to get ready, but now it seems easy.

The day before the test I was pretty nervous. It was hard to concentrate at work, so I left early and went to the testing center. I wanted to make sure I could find it.

Then I went home and reviewed the writing process one last time. Willie fixed me a nice supper, and we went to bed early. Before I went to bed, I got all of my things ready for the big day.

The next morning, I got up, ate a good breakfast, and went to the testing center. I took the lunch Willie packed for me. I stopped and got a candy bar to eat during a break in the test. Then I went in and took the test. I began to panic but some calming thoughts helped me to get focused. And I passed! I just got the scores in the mail. Let's all go out and celebrate next weekend when you are in town.

Love,

Cindy

Answer the following questions:

1. What did Cindy do to get ready for the GED Test?

2. What can you do to get ready for the GED Test?

Getting Ready for the Test

Taking a test like the GED is an important event. You should plan carefully for the day of the test. Here are some ideas that will help you do your best on any part of the GED Test.

The Week Before the Test . . .

- Find out the location of the testing center. If possible, go there before the test. Ask where to park the day of the test if you will be driving. If you are taking public transportation, find the best route.

- Make sure you have all the things required for the test, such as your driver's license or other ID, a watch, and some pens and pencils.

The Night Before the Test . . .

- Make sure everything you need for the test is ready and organized.

- If the test is early in the morning, lay out your clothes and set an alarm clock.

- Make sure your car keys, bus pass, or bus fare are ready.

- Do not try to cram. You might briefly review important concepts, such as the writing process, but do not stay up late studying. Instead, go to bed early and get plenty of sleep.

The Day of the Test . . .

- Eat breakfast.

- Take some fruit, nuts, or candy with you to eat during breaks.

- Think calm thoughts all day.

- Arrive for the test a few minutes early.

During the Test . . .

- Before you begin, think positive thoughts. Concentrate for a moment on all the time and energy you have spent preparing for the test.

- If you find yourself getting nervous, stop for a few minutes to think relaxing thoughts. Take a few deep breaths.

After the Test . . .

- Get some rest.

- Do something fun to reward yourself for all of your hard work. Go out to dinner with your family. Take your kids to the park. Buy yourself a small present.

When You Get Your Results . . .

- If you passed, reward yourself again. Do something fun.

- If you need to retake any part of the test, determine the areas you need to review. If you need extra essay-writing practice, answer one of the Additional Essay Topics on page 240. Evaluate your writing using the GED Essay Scoring Guide on the inside front cover. Then make a plan to review the areas where your writing needs extra help.

Planning Your Time

Since you have only 45 minutes to write your GED essay, you need to plan your time wisely. Here is how Cindy planned her time:

Gathering Ideas:	10 minutes
Organizing:	5 minutes
Writing:	20 minutes
Revising:	10 minutes
Total:	45 minutes

Now you do it. Think about your experiences using the writing process in this book and complete the chart below.

Gathering Ideas: _____

Organizing: _____

Writing: _____

Revising: _____

Total: _____

Make sure the time adds up to 45 minutes.

WRITING A GED ESSAY: *Taking the Test*

- Prepare yourself for taking the test during the days before the test.

- If you feel nervous during the test, think calming thoughts.

- Make a plan for using your time wisely during the test. Keep track of the time while you write.

GED Practice

Part A

Directions: Use the form below to plan your time for the writing process.

Gathering Ideas: _____

Organizing: _____

Writing: _____

Revising: _____

Total: _____

Part B

Directions: Use the four steps of the writing process to write an essay that responds to the following GED essay topic. Follow the steps below. Keep track of the time you started, and try to stick to your plan for using your time.

――――――――――― T O P I C ―――――――――――

What are the qualities of a true friend?

In your essay, list the qualities you think are important in a true friend. Explain why these qualities are so important. Use your personal observations, experience, and knowledge.

1. **Gather Ideas**

   Read the essay topic, decide how you will respond to the question, and think of the main idea for your essay. Write the type of writing and your main idea on the lines below. Then, on a separate sheet of paper, gather ideas for your essay.

   Type of writing: _____

   Main idea: _____

2. **Organize Your Ideas**

   Put the ideas you gathered in the order in which you will write about them. Make sure that all the ideas are relevant. Cross off any ideas that are not relevant.

3. **Write Your Essay**

   Use your organized ideas to write an essay on a separate sheet of paper. Do not spend a lot of time worrying about grammar, punctuation, or spelling. You will check for mistakes after you write your essay.

4. **Revise Your Essay**

   Check the information, the organization, and the language you used for grammar and spelling.

Part C

Directions: Review your plan for using your time. Do you need to adjust the allocation? Revise your plan if you want to.

Gathering Ideas: _____

Organizing: _____

Writing: _____

Revising: _____

Total: _____

Answers are on page 280.

Writing and Life

Directions: Use the four steps of the writing process and your writing plan to write an essay that responds to the following topic. Write your essay on a separate sheet of paper.

TOPIC

What can people do to increase their life expectancy?

In your essay, list what people can do to live longer. Explain why it will increase life expectancy. Use your personal observations, experience, and knowledge.

Answers are on page 280.

Self-Assessment

Part A

Directions: Ask your instructor or a friend to score your essays using the GED Essay Scoring Guide on the inside front cover of this book.

Part B

Directions: Make any final revisions to your plan for using your time.

Gathering Ideas: _____

Organizing: _____

Writing: _____

Revising: _____

Total: _____

Answers are on page 280.

Language Arts, Writing, Part II

Essay Directions and Topic

Look at the box on page 234. In the box is your assigned topic.

You must write on the assigned topic ONLY.

You will have 45 minutes to write on your assigned essay topic. If you run out of time, note where you were in your essay. Then complete the essay. This will help you determine how much faster you need to work to complete your essay in 45 minutes.

Your essay will be scored according to its overall effectiveness. The score will be based on the following features:

- Well-focused main points

- Clear organization

- Specific development of your ideas

- Control of sentence structure, punctuation, grammar, word choice, and spelling

As you work, be sure to do the following:

- Write legibly in ink so your instructor will be able to read your writing.

- Write on the assigned topic. If you write on a topic other than the one assigned, your essay will not be scored.

- Write your essay on a separate sheet of lined paper.

Go on to the next page.

POSTTEST

What is the best decision you ever made?

In your essay, identify that decision. Explain why it is the best decision you ever made. Use your personal observations, experience, and knowledge.

Part II of the Language Arts, Writing Test is a test to determine how well you can use written language to explain your ideas.

In preparing your essay, you should take the following steps:

- Read the **DIRECTIONS** and the **TOPIC** carefully.

- Plan your essay before you write. Use scratch paper to make any notes. These notes will not be scored.

- After you finish writing your essay, reread what you have written and make any changes that will improve your essay.

Evaluation guidelines are on page 235.

POSTTEST

Evaluation Guidelines

If possible, ask your instructor or another student to give your essay an overall score using the GED Essay Scoring Guide. If you have to score your own essay, let your essay sit for a few days and then score it.

Overall score: _____

Now look at the GED Essay Scoring Guide on the inside front cover of this book. Give your essay a score of 1–4 for each area of the scoring guide. Write the score for each area in the "Score" column of the chart below. For each score of 2 or less, pay attention to the information in the "Instruction" column.

Criteria	Score	Instruction
Response to the Prompt		Review the *Learning to Write* sections in this book.
Organization		Review the *Expanding Ideas* sections in this book.
Development and Details		Review the *Expanding Ideas* sections in this book.
Conventions of Edited American English (EAE)		Review the *Looking at Language* sections in this book.
Word Choice		Review the *Looking at Language* sections in this book.

Essay Directions and Topic

Look at the box on page 238. In the box is your assigned topic.

You must write on the assigned topic ONLY.

You will have 45 minutes to write on your assigned essay topic. If you run out of time, note where you were in your essay. Then complete the essay. This will help you determine how much faster you need to work to complete your essay in 45 minutes.

Your essay will be scored according to its overall effectiveness. The score will be based on the following features:

- Well-focused main points

- Clear organization

- Specific development of your ideas

- Control of sentence structure, punctuation, grammar, word choice, and spelling

As you work, be sure to do the following:

- Write legibly <u>in ink</u> so your instructor will be able to read your writing.

- Write on the assigned topic. If you write on a topic other than the one assigned, your essay will not be scored.

- Write your essay on a separate sheet of lined paper.

Go on to the next page.

PRACTICE TEST

TOPIC

How will a GED certificate benefit your life?

In your essay, list the benefits of obtaining a GED certificate. Explain why it will benefit your life. Use your personal observations, experience, and knowledge.

Part II of the Language Arts, Writing Test is a test to determine how well you can use written language to explain your ideas.

In preparing your essay, you should take the following steps:

- Read the **DIRECTIONS** and the **TOPIC** carefully.

- Plan your essay before you write. Use scratch paper to make any notes. These notes will not be scored.

- After you finish writing your essay, reread what you have written and make any changes that will improve your essay.

Evaluation guidelines are on page 239.

PRACTICE TEST
Evaluation Guidelines

If possible, ask your instructor or another student to give your essay an overall score using the GED Essay Scoring Guide. If you have to score your own essay, let your essay sit for a few days and then score it.

Overall score: _____

Now look at the GED Essay Scoring Guide on the inside front cover of this book. Give your essay a score of 1–4 for each area of the scoring guide. Write the score for each area in the "Score" column of the chart below. For each score of 2 or less, pay attention to the information in the "Instruction" column.

Criteria	Score	Instruction
Response to the Prompt		Review the *Learning to Write* sections in this book.
Organization		Review the *Expanding Ideas* sections in this book.
Development and Details		Review the *Expanding Ideas* sections in this book.
Conventions of Edited American English (EAE)		Review the *Looking at Language* sections in this book.
Word Choice		Review the *Looking at Language* sections in this book.

Additional Essay Topics

Directions: Respond to the following GED essay topics to get additional practice. Be sure to follow the steps of the writing process to develop a strong essay for each topic. Try to complete each essay in 45 minutes. Use the GED Essay Scoring Guide to evaluate your work.

--- **T O P I C** ---

What is your best quality?

In your essay, identify that quality and explain why it is your best. Use your personal observations, experience, and knowledge.

--- **T O P I C** ---

There are many simple things people can do to safeguard their health.

Write an essay explaining how people can begin to protect their health without drastically changing their lifestyle.

--- **T O P I C** ---

What is the best way to combat stress?

In your essay, describe what you do to combat stress. Explain why it helps to decrease stress. Use your personal observations, experience, and knowledge.

Writing Handbook

- Organization

- Sentence Structure

- Usage

- Mechanics

Introduction

As you worked through this book, you learned many skills and strategies to help you write a well-developed essay for Part II of the Language Arts, Writing Test. However, many of the skills you learned for improving your writing will also help you to succeed on the other half of the test.

The chart on the next page lists the main errors you will find on Part I of the Language Arts, Writing Test.

The following pages contain a brief review of the skills and strategies that will help you succeed on both parts of the Language Arts, Writing Test.

Type of Error	Example	Correction
ORGANIZATION		
Improper text division	A paragraph contains two main ideas.	Split the paragraph into two paragraphs, each containing a main idea.
Lack of a topic sentence	A paragraph does not contain a topic sentence.	Choose an appropriate topic sentence that relates to the other sentences in the paragraph.
Lack of unity or coherence	A sentence in a paragraph does not have the same tone as the rest of the paragraph or does not relate to the main idea of the paragraph.	Revise the sentence to fit with the rest of the paragraph, or eliminate it.
SENTENCE STRUCTURE		
Sentence fragment	Because it was a holiday.	Because it was a holiday, **the children did not have to go to school.**
Run-on sentence or comma splice	He left early, we met him at the train.	He left early, **so** we met him at the train.
Wordy or repetitive sentence	I went to the grocery store to buy some milk, and I went to the grocery store to buy some eggs.	I went to the grocery store **to buy some milk and eggs.**
Incorrect coordination or subordination	Computers are easy to use, so people are afraid of them.	Computers are easy to use, **but** people are afraid of them.
Misplaced or dangling modifier	Sitting in front of the television, her eyes became glassy.	**As she sat in front of the television,** her eyes became glassy.
Lack of parallel structure	The report is intended to inform, amuse, and being instructional.	The report is intended to inform, amuse, **and instruct.**
USAGE		
Subject-verb disagreement	Jim and Raoul was at the meeting today.	Jim and Raoul **were** at the meeting today.
Incorrect verb tense	Tomorrow, the fun was just getting started.	Tomorrow, the fun **will just be** getting started.
Pronoun-antecedent disagreement	Everyone should bring their driver's license.	Everyone should bring his or her driver's license.
MECHANICS		
Incorrect capitalization	The country of south africa is South of the equator.	The country of **South Africa** is **south** of the equator.
Improper comma usage	Whenever we see each other we are surprised.	Whenever we see each other**,** we are surprised.
Misspelled homonym, possessive, or contraction	They took they're film to the convenience store.	They took **their** film to the convenience store.

Organization

The following skills will help you with paragraph and essay organization.

Combining Paragraphs

Sometimes a writer unnecessarily creates a new paragraph. If the new paragraph supports the topic sentence of the previous paragraph, the two paragraphs need to be combined.

(A)

This fall, I was sick twice. In October I caught a cold because I got wet on my way home from work. While I was on the bus, it suddenly began to pour down rain. When I got off the bus, I stepped directly in a deep puddle that soaked my shoes. Since my umbrella was at home, I had no choice but to walk home in the pouring rain.

(B)

By the time I got there I was completely soaked, and I caught a terrible cold. I had a cough, a runny nose, and a sore throat. I was sick for a week and missed two days of work.

(C)

The second time I got sick was in November. I had to work a double shift. I got really tired, and when I got home I had a fever and a sore throat. The next day, I had the flu so bad that I could hardly get out of bed. That time I missed work for a week.

In the previous passage, paragraphs A and B need to be combined. They are both about the same main idea: the cold the writer caught in October.

(A)

This fall, I was sick twice. In October I caught a cold because I got wet on my way home from work. While I was on the bus, it suddenly began to pour down rain. When I got off the bus, I stepped directly in a deep puddle that soaked my shoes. Since my umbrella was at home, I had no choice but to walk home in the pouring rain. **By the time I got there I was completely soaked, and I caught a terrible cold. I had a cough, a runny nose, and a sore throat. I was sick for a week and missed two days of work.**

(B)

The second time I got sick was in November. I had to work a double shift. I got really tired, and when I got home I had a fever and a sore throat. The next day, I had the flu so bad that I could hardly get out of bed. That time I missed work for a week.

Deleting Sentences

Sometimes a writer includes an idea in a paragraph that is not about the main idea. This sentence does not belong in the paragraph and needs to be removed.

Lately I have noticed a number of safety issues that are a hazard for all employees. First, there is no running at any time. Second, all employees in the manufacturing area must wear safety glasses at all times. Operators of drill presses must wear goggles. **We need to organize the tools in the woodworking area.** Third, everyone in the warehouse and factory must wear either safety shoes or boots with steel toes. There are no exceptions to these rules.

In the paragraph above, the sentence about organizing tools does not belong. While this sentence may be true and about work, it is not about safety at work, which is the main idea of the paragraph.

Dividing Paragraphs

A good paragraph should contain only one main idea.

Last spring was really wonderful. My family and I went camping in Texas for a week. We went hiking several times and saw some beautiful, rugged scenery. We loved the Texas coast, and we went fishing several times. However, we never caught anything. Then in the winter we went to Florida for Christmas. My parents live there now, so my husband and I and our three kids drove down after school got out. It took two days. We had fun swimming at the beach. We also went to the Everglades. We saw several alligators. We went fishing there, too, because my husband and my father both love to fish. This time we were luckier, and we had fresh fish for dinner almost every night.

The paragraph above has two main ideas. It tells about two wonderful trips—one to Texas and one to Florida. The way to fix the problem is to divide the paragraph into two, so that one paragraph is about the trip to Texas and the other is about the trip to Florida.

Last spring was really wonderful. My family and I went camping in Texas for a week. We went hiking several times and saw some beautiful, rugged scenery. We loved the Texas coast, and we went fishing several times. However, we never caught anything.

Then in the winter we went to Florida for Christmas. My parents live there now, so my husband and I and our three kids drove down after school got out. It took two days. We had fun swimming at the beach. We also went to the Everglades. We saw several alligators. We went fishing there, too, because my husband and my father both love to fish. This time we were luckier, and we had fresh fish for dinner almost every night.

Sequence Words

A good essay contains **sequence words** to help the reader make the transition from one step or event to the next. These words include ordinal numbers (*first, second, third, fourth*) and adverbs of sequence (*next, then, finally,* and *last*). When these words come at the beginning of a sentence, they are followed by a comma.

> You should **first** get out four hamburger buns. **Second,** spread mustard on the top of each bun. **Third,** put a slice of turkey and a slice of Swiss cheese in each bun. **Then,** wrap each bun in a sheet of aluminum foil. **Next,** put the sandwiches on a baking sheet and put them in a 350-degree oven for 20 minutes. **Finally,** remove the sandwiches from the oven and serve them piping hot.

Thesis Statement

In an essay, a good introductory paragraph ends with a **thesis statement**, a statement of what is to follow in the body paragraphs.

> I must say that I really do not practice many sports. I do not like to run, and I really do not like games such as baseball or basketball. However, I know that exercise is an important part of staying healthy. That's why I try to walk as much as possible. **Walking is my favorite sport because it's easy to incorporate into my day and provides exercise and relaxation.**

The thesis statement above indicates that the body paragraphs are going to give information on why walking is an easy way to get exercise and to relax.

Tone

The **tone** of a good paragraph or essay needs to be consistent throughout. The tone of a piece of writing refers to the style in which it is written. Tone can be formal, friendly, funny, serious, and so on, but it must be consistent. The tone of a piece of writing should not change suddenly. For example, if you are writing a formal business letter, you do not want to interrupt it unexpectedly with an informal exclamation. Likewise, if you are writing a friendly note to a relative, you do not want to close with a formal sentence.

> Barrington bats are the best softball bats you can buy. Imagine you're up to bat. Your team has players on second and third. A perfect pitch comes right across home plate. Luckily, you're holding a Barrington softball bat, specially designed for peak performance. CRACK! You hit a perfect fly deep into center field! The fielder can't catch it on the fly. By the time the fielder gets the ball, two runners have made it home and you're on second base! **For this reason, you and your associates need to consider buying a Barrington softball bat at your earliest convenience.** Buy a Barrington bat! It's the bat of champion softball teams!

The tone of the paragraph above is was informal. The sentence in boldface does not fit with the rest of the paragraph. Its tone is too formal.

Topic Sentence

A good paragraph begins with a **topic sentence** that states the main idea of the paragraph.

> **I like walking because it's an easy way to get some relaxation and exercise.** On nice days I simply walk to work. I also walk as much as possible while shopping. If I am going to the mall, I try to park far from the mall entrance and then walk to the door, in order to get exercise. I always take the stairs rather than the elevator or escalator at work and at the mall. That way I get some extra exercise, too. I use the extra time to relax my mind and think peaceful thoughts or to plan my free time. That way, I can relax a little. One day I figured that if I walk to work three times a week, park far from store entrances, and always take the stairs, I get about five hours of exercise a week. That is pretty good—and it helps me keep my weight down and my muscles strong.

The topic sentence above gives a good indication of the content of the paragraph.

Organization

Sentence Structure

The following skills will help you with basic sentence structure.

Adjectives and Adverbs

An **adjective** gives more information about a noun or pronoun. An **adverb** gives more information about a verb or adjective. Many adverbs end in *ly*.

> He has a **slow** car. *(ADJECTIVE)*
>
> He **slowly** drove home. *(ADVERB)*
>
> He is **very** busy today. *(ADVERB)*

Some adjectives and adverbs have the same form.

> She always drives **fast**. *(ADVERB)*
>
> She's a **fast** driver. *(ADJECTIVE)*

Not all words that end in *ly* are adverbs.

> She's a **lovely** person.

Appositives

An **appositive** is a noun phrase that gives more information about another noun. Appositives are usually set off by commas.

> My dog, **Abby,** is a faithful companion.
>
> Max, **my cat,** has a beautiful furry coat.

Complete Sentences

A **complete sentence** has a subject and a verb. A sentence that lacks a subject or a verb is called a **fragment**.

> **FRAGMENT:** My husband and I to the movies almost every weekend.
>
> **COMPLETE SENTENCE:** My mother baby-sits for us.

Complex Sentences

Two related sentences can be combined to form a longer sentence.

> She didn't hit the brakes in time. She hit the car in front of her.

BECOMES

> She hit the car in front of her because she didn't hit the brakes in time.

The conjunction *because* joins the two sentences, which become **clauses** of a larger sentence. The second clause *(because she didn't hit the brakes in time)* cannot stand alone as a sentence. For this reason it is called a **dependent clause**. The first clause *(She hit the car in front of her)* can stand alone as a sentence. It is an **independent clause**.

A **complex sentence** consists of an independent clause and a dependent clause joined by a conjunction. The conjunctions that join the clauses in complex sentences are called **subordinating conjunctions**. Common subordinating conjunctions include *when, while, although, because, since, so that,* and *in order that.*

When the dependent clause comes first in a complex sentence, a comma must come after the dependent clause. If the independent clause comes first, a comma is not necessary.

Compound Sentences

Two related sentences can be combined to form a longer sentence.

> She didn't hit the brakes in time. She hit the car in front of her.

BECOMES

> She didn't hit the brakes in time, and she hit the car in front of her.

OR

> She didn't hit the brakes in time, so she hit the car in front of her.

Both of these longer sentences use **coordinating conjunctions** *(and* and *so)* to join the smaller sentences. Common coordinating conjunctions include *and, but, yet, or, nor, for,* and *so.*

The two smaller sentences become clauses of the larger sentence. A **clause** is a group of words with a subject and verb that is part of a larger sentence. Because each clause in the preceding example can stand alone as a sentence, the clauses are called **independent clauses.** A **compound sentence** consists of two independent clauses joined with a coordinating conjunction.

When a coordinating conjunction is used to join independent clauses, a comma must separate the clauses.

> She was driving very quickly, for she was late for a doctor's appointment.

Sentence Structure

Dangling Modifiers

A **dangling modifier** is a modifier that has no clear reference in a sentence.

Barking wildly, the thief was scared off.

To make the sentence correct, the dangling modifier needs to be changed to a dependent clause.

Because the dog was barking wildly, the thief ran away.

The sentence can also be rewritten entirely.

Barking wildly, the dog scared off the thief.

Linking Verbs

Linking verbs are used to link the subject with a word that tells more about it—usually an adjective and/or another noun. Common linking verbs are *be (is, are), seem, sound, look, feel, taste, smell,* and *become.*

A Mustang **is** a sleek car.

That car **looks** speedy.

Linking verbs are usually used in the simple present, past, and future tenses and in the present perfect tense.

The soup **tasted** delicious.

An exception is the verb *become*. It can be used in the progressive tense when it is describing a change someone is experiencing.

He is in medical school. He **is becoming** a cancer specialist.

Misplaced Modifiers

Sometimes a modifying phrase is not placed near the noun it modifies. This phrase is called a **misplaced modifier**.

The car hit a tree driving over the curb.

In the sentence above, the modifier *driving over the curb* is misplaced. The sentence seems to say that the tree was driving, which is impossible. The sentence needs to be rearranged to make sense.

Driving over the curb, the car hit a tree.

OR

The car hit a tree when it drove over the curb.

Parallel Structure

Conjunctions such as *and* or *but* are often used to connect a series of elements, such as nouns, verbs, and phrases.

> People should stop smoking immediately because it's unattractive, expensive, and dangerous.

> Smokers often spend money on lighters, matches, and ashtrays.

The connected elements in each sentence are in the same grammatical form—in other words they have **parallel structure**. In the first sentence, the parallel elements are adjectives. In the second sentence, they are nouns.

The following sentence does not have parallel structure.

> Sean quit smoking, started exercising, and to begin eating healthfully.

The first two connected elements contain verbs in the past tense—*quit* and *started*, while the third element contains an infinitive—*to begin*. The sentence can be corrected by using the past tense for all three elements.

> Sean **quit** smoking, **started** exercising, and **began** eating healthfully.

Prepositional Phrases

A **prepositional phrase** consists of a preposition and a noun.

> **To this day,** dogs perform many valuable services.

> Cats often look at you **in a condescending manner.**

A comma must be used to set off these phrases when they come at the beginning of a sentence.

> **NO COMMA:** He answered the question **in an angry tone of voice.**

> **COMMA: In an angry tone of voice,** he answered the question.

Run-on Sentences, Comma Splices, and Fragments

A **run-on sentence** consists of two clauses that are not joined with a conjunction.

> He got up early he wanted to go for a run in the park.

To fix a run-on, add a conjunction (and a comma, if necessary).

> He got up early **because** he wanted to go for a run in the park.

A **comma splice** is similar to a run-on. It consists of two clauses joined only by a comma.

> He got up early, he could go for a run.

To fix a comma splice, add a conjunction (and a comma, if necessary).

> He got up early**, so** he could go for a run.

A dependent clause cannot stand alone as a sentence. A dependent clause that stands alone is called a **fragment**.

> Because he needed to earn some extra spending money for the holidays.

One way to correct a fragment is to delete the subordinating conjunction.

> He needed to earn some extra money for the holidays.

Another way to correct a fragment is to join it to another clause.

> He got a part-time job because he needed to earn some extra money for the holidays.

Sentence Structure

Sentence Combining

Short, choppy sentences can be combined into a compound or a complex sentence.

> I clocked out of work. I went to the mall.

> I clocked out of work, and I went to the mall. **(COMPOUND)**

> After I clocked out of work, I went to the mall. **(COMPLEX)**

A **compound sentence** has two **independent clauses** joined by the **coordinating conjunction** *and*. The clauses are independent because they can stand alone as complete sentences.

A **complex sentence** has a **dependent clause** and an independent clause. In the complex sentence above, the first clause *(After I clocked out of work)* is the dependent clause. The other clause *(I went to the mall)* is the independent clause. Words such as *when, while, before,* and *after* are examples of **subordinating conjunctions** used to join two clauses. Sentences with subordinating conjunctions often help to show the relationship among past events.

> **After** we ate lunch, the boys took naps.

> I wrote postcards **while** they were sleeping.

REMEMBER: if the dependent clause precedes the independent clause, the two clauses must be separated by a comma.

Subjects and Verbs

The **subject** of a sentence tells *who* or *what* the sentence is about. The **verb** tells what the subject *is* or *does*.

> Mr. Smith is an excellent fisherman.
> SUBJECT   VERB

> Last week he caught ten trout.
> SUBJECT VERB

> He doesn't fish on weekdays.
> SUBJECT   VERB

Sentence Structure

Subordinating Conjunctions

A **subordinating conjunction** is used to join a dependent clause to an independent clause in a complex sentence.

> People should stop smoking **because** it is harmful to their health.

> **If** pregnant women smoke, they may cause harm to their unborn children.

The following chart contains a list of common subordinating conjunctions.

Subordinating Conjunction	Meaning	Example
after as long as as soon as before until when whenever while	To show time	She answered the questions **as soon as** she finished reading the chapter. **Before** you start to paint, you should cover all the furniture. I get very cranky **when** I don't have my morning cup of coffee.
because in order that since so that	To show cause and effect or purpose	People should stop smoking **because** it can cause cancer. **Since** Jasmine won't be able to attend, we will only have five guests.
if unless whether	To show a condition	**If** you can't attend, please call me. Jorge will go running tomorrow morning **unless** it is raining.
although even though though whereas	To show contrast	**Even though** she woke up early, Becky was still late for class. Evan chose a black suit **whereas** Jordan chose a blue one.
as if as though	To show similarity	He ate **as though** he hadn't seen food in a month.
where wherever	To show place	She will do **whatever** needs to be done.

Unclear Pronouns

Pronouns can be used in place of nouns to make writing less repetitive. However, pronouns should always have a clear **antecedent**. The reader should be able to tell exactly to *whom* or *what* each pronoun refers.

> **CLEAR:** I found the missing purse and gave it to the woman who lost it.

> **UNCLEAR:** While Bill was talking to Mr. Maguire, he got angry.

The second sentence has an unclear pronoun. It is not clear whether *he* refers to Bill or Mr. Maguire. In the first sentence, the pronoun *it* has a clear reference—*purse.*

When a pronoun is unclear, it should be replaced with a noun, or rewritten in a way that is clearer.

> While he was talking to Mr. Maguire, **Bill** got angry.

Sometimes a pronoun has no clear antecedent, or noun to refer to.

> **UNCLEAR:** We need to fight poverty and injustice in the world so that they have the opportunity to get ahead and succeed in life.

> **CLEAR:** I wrote to my senators and representatives to express my ideas, and they responded to my letters right away.

The first sentence contains a pronoun with no clear antecedent. It is unclear to whom the word *they* refers in this sentence. It could refer to people in third world countries, to unemployed youth in the United States, or to some other group. The unclear pronoun needs to be replaced with a more specific noun:

> We need to fight poverty and injustice in the world so that **people in all countries** have the opportunity to get ahead and succeed in life.

Verbal Phrases

A **verbal phrase** uses a verb form to describe a noun. Verbal phrases can end with *ed* or *ing.*

> **Staying beside her owner,** Abby ran through the park.

> **Worried and confused,** the dog howled through the night.

Usage

The following skills will help you with verb tense and use.

Imperatives

An **imperative** is a command. It is formed by using the base form of the verb without a subject. The subject of an imperative is always understood to be *you*.

> (You) **Put** a quarter in the gum machine. Then (you) **turn** the handle.

Past Continuing Tense

The **past continuing tense** is used for actions that continued in the past. The past continuing tense is formed with a helping verb (a form of *have, do,* or *be*) plus the base verb ending in *ing*.

> We **were living** on Green Street.

> She **was working** at Broadway Convenience Store.

Simple Past Tense

The **simple past tense** is used for actions that happened at a specific time in the past.

> She arrived at 6 P.M.

> She left at 7 P.M.

The simple past tense of regular verbs is formed by adding *ed* or *d* to the base form of the verb.

- Add *d* to regular verbs that end in *e:*

  bake   **baked**

- Add *ed* to the base form of all other regular verbs:

  start   **started**

  cook   **cooked**

- For verbs that end in a consonant and *y*, change the *y* to *i* and add *ed:*

  study   **studied**

- For verbs that end in a vowel and *y*, add *ed:*

  stay   stayed

- For negatives, use *did not* and the base form of the verb:

  did not bake

  did not start

  did not stay

English has a number of verbs that are irregular in the simple past tense. These verbs are irregular only in the affirmative. The negative is formed with *did not* and the base form of the verb.

go	**went**	**did not go**
buy	**bought**	**did not buy**
catch	**caught**	**did not catch**

The simple past tense of *be* is *was/were:*

She **was** late yesterday.

They **were** on time this morning.

Simple Present Tense

The **simple present tense** is used to show habitual or regular actions.

She always puts the garbage out on Monday morning.

He always presses the fifth floor button when he enters the elevator.

The simple present tense is formed by using the base form of the verb (the verb without any ending), such as *put* and *press*, or by adding a final *s* or *es*, such as *puts* or *presses*. In general, verbs that end in a "hissing" sound *(s, sh, ch, x,* and *z)* take the *es* ending. Look at the following chart:

Subject	Verb
I, you, we, they	**put, press**
he, she, it	**puts, presses**

Usage

Mechanics

The following skills will help you with mechanics.

Capital Letters

A sentence always begins with a capital letter.

> **She** really enjoys working on her car.

The pronoun *I* should always be written as a capital letter.

> Joe and **I** like to watch TV late at night.

Proper nouns and adjectives should always be capitalized. A **proper noun** is the name of a specific person, place, or thing. A **proper adjective** is an adjective formed from a proper noun, like *Mexican*.

> I think that **Tyrice** wants to travel to **Mexico** some day.

> She loves to eat **Mexican** food.

End Punctuation

Every sentence should end with a question mark, exclamation point, or period.

Every question should end with a question mark.

> What is your favorite pastime**?**

> Do you sing in a choir**?**

An **exclamation** shows great interest or emotion. An exclamation point should be used to end an exclamation.

> It costs $100**!**

> What a great movie**!**

A period should be used to end sentences that are not questions or exclamations. Periods are used in abbreviations too.

> Her name is Dr**.** Christine Johnson**.**

Homonyms

Homonyms are words that sound the same but have different spellings or meanings. Using the correct spelling is important on the Language Arts, Writing Test because homonym errors are very confusing to readers.

> **INCORRECT:**   Good to **meat** you.

> **CORRECT:**   Good to **meet** you.

GED Connection

Directions: Choose the <u>one best answer</u> to each question. Some of the sentences may contain errors in organization, sentence structure, usage, and mechanics. A few sentences, however, may be correct as written. Read the sentences carefully and then answer the questions based on them. For each question, choose the answer that would result in the most effective writing of the sentence or sentences.

Questions 1–9 refer to the following memo.

To: All Employees

From: Edward Janssen

Re: Mail Services Safety

(A)

(1) In recent weeks, one of the biggest concerns at Coretech, Inc. have been the continued safety of employees with respect to mail and packages. (2) We have received a number of reports involving suspicious mail, and these reports have been investigated. (3) To date, these reports have not led to the discovery of any abnormal mail contents.

(B)

(4) To enhance safety in regard to mail delivery, coretech is taking the following steps:

- (5) All incoming mail will be rigorously inspected by mailroom staff wearing protective gear. (6) Suspicious mail was set aside for appropriate handling.

- (7) All deliveries sent by messenger will go to the mailroom for inspection, prior to delivery to the recipient. (8) The same policy will apply to deliveries sent by other private delivery services.

(C)

(9) Please follow these guidelines:

- (10) Use e-mail or fax rather than mail/overnight delivery service whenever possible.

- (11) When sending out mail, make sure they are clearly marked with both a delivery and a return address.

- (12) Encountering suspicious mail, your manager must be notified immediately.

(D)

(13) Please be assured that Coretech will continue to monitor mail service policies and revising procedures as circumstances require.

1. **Sentence 1: In recent weeks, one of the biggest concerns at Coretech, Inc. have been the continued safety of employees with respect to mail and packages.**

   What correction should be made to sentence 1?

   (1) remove the comma after *weeks*
   (2) insert a comma after *employees*
   (3) change *have been* to *will have been*
   (4) change *have* to *has*
   (5) no correction is necessary

2. **Sentence 2: We have received a number of reports involving suspicious mail, and these reports have been investigated.**

   The most effective revision of sentence 2 would begin with which group of words?

   (1) These reports have been investigated and received
   (2) We have received and investigated a number of reports
   (3) Investigating a number of reports, we have received
   (4) Reports involving suspicious mail have been received
   (5) Suspicious mail has been received, and these reports

3. **Sentence 4: To enhance safety in regard to mail delivery, coretech is taking the following steps:**

   What correction should be made to sentence 4?

   (1) remove the comma after *delivery*
   (2) change *is taking* to *will have been taking*
   (3) change *mail* to *male*
   (4) change *coretech* to *Coretech*
   (5) no correction is necessary

4. **Sentence 6: Suspicious mail <u>was set aside</u> for appropriate handling.**

   Which is the best way to write the underlined portion of the text? If the original is the best way, choose option (1).

   (1) was set aside
   (2) were set aside
   (3) to be set aside
   (4) are set aside
   (5) will be set aside

5. **Sentences 7 and 8: All deliveries sent by messenger will go to the mailroom for inspection, prior to delivery to the recipient. The same policy will apply to deliveries sent by other private delivery services.**

    The most effective combination of sentences 7 and 8 would include which group of words?

    (1) All deliveries sent by messenger and other private delivery services
    (2) Deliveries sent by messenger and deliveries sent by other private delivery services
    (3) will go to the mailroom for inspection, and the same policy will apply
    (4) Other private delivery services and all deliveries sent by messenger apply
    (5) Prior to delivery from other private delivery services,

6. Which sentence below would be most effective at the beginning of paragraph C?

    (1) Building security is also very important.
    (2) If you receive suspicious mail, you should follow a plan of action.
    (3) While Coretech is taking these steps, we are asking you to be vigilant and to take an active role in controlling the flow of outgoing and incoming mail.
    (4) Do not send or receive personal mail in the office.
    (5) Coretech is not responsible for any mail that does not go through the mailroom.

7. **Sentence 11: When sending out mail, make sure they are clearly marked with both a delivery and a return address.**

    What correction should be made to sentence 11?

    (1) insert a comma after *marked*
    (2) change *they are* to *it is*
    (3) change *they are* to *they were*
    (4) remove the comma after *mail*
    (5) no correction is necessary

8. **Sentence 12: <u>Encountering suspicious mail</u>, your manager must be notified immediately.**

   Which is the best way to write the underlined portion of the text? If the original is the best way, choose option (1).

   (1) Encountering suspicious mail
   (2) While encountering suspicious mail
   (3) If you encounter suspicious mail
   (4) As soon as you encounter suspicious mail
   (5) Suspicious mail is encountered and

9. **Sentence 13: Please be assured that Coretech will continue to monitor mail service policies and revising procedures as circumstances require.**

   The most effective revision of sentence 13 would include which group of words?

   (1) continuing to monitor mail service policies and revising procedures
   (2) monitoring mail service policies and revising procedures
   (3) mail service policies as well as revising procedures
   (4) Assuring that Coretech will continue,
   (5) continue to monitor mail service policies and revise procedures

Questions 10–16 refer to the following instructions.

Cooking a Turkey

(A)

(1) Its holiday time, and the experts at Turkey Talk are here to offer you some hints on cooking that delicious meal you have been dreaming about. (2) With a little bit of advance planning and some extra time in the kitchen, you can impress your family and guests and treat them to the meal of a lifetime. (3) Just follow the steps outlined below and call 1-800-TURKEYS for additional information.

(B)

(4) After preheating your oven to 325 degrees, take the turkey from the refrigerator, and remove the plastic wrappings. (5) While the oven heats up, the turkey can come a bit closer to room temperature. (6) Next, remove the giblets and neck from the turkey's main cavity. (7) If the turkey was very juicy, pat it dry with paper towels.

(C)

(8) Your next step is to stuff the turkey. (9) Stuff the main cavity first but do not pack it too tightly. (10) Overstuffing a turkey can result in soggy pasty, and undercooked stuffing. (11) If you are not using stuffing, you can add some herbs or vegetables to the cavity to improve the flavor of the meet. (12) You can also add herbs and vegetables to the gravy to increase its flavor. (13) Next, skewers to fasten the flap of skin over the cavity. (14) Metal or wood are a good material for the skewers. (15) Tie the legs together with cotton string. (16) As a final step, rub the turkey all over with vegetable oil or butter to create a crispy, brown skin while roasting.

10. **Sentence 1: Its holiday time, and the experts at Turkey Talk are here to offer you some hints on cooking that delicious meal you have been dreaming about.**

    Which is the best way to write the underlined portion of the text? If the original is the best way, choose option (1).

    (1) Its holiday time, and
    (2) It's holiday time, and
    (3) Its holiday time and
    (4) Its holiday time, but
    (5) Its Holiday time, and

11. **Sentence 4: After preheating your oven to 325 degrees, take the turkey from the refrigerator, and remove the plastic wrappings.**

    If you rewrote sentence 4 beginning with

    Before you begin,

    the next word(s) should be

    (1) preheat your oven to 325 degrees,
    (2) after preheating your oven to 325 degrees
    (3) preheat, take, and remove the turkey
    (4) taking the turkey from the refrigerator and removing the plastic wrappings
    (5) to preheat your oven and take the turkey from the refrigerator,

12. **Sentence 7: If the turkey <u>was very juicy</u>, pat it dry with paper towels.**

    Which is the best way to write the underlined portion of the text? If the original is the best way, choose option (1).

    (1) was very juicy
    (2) is very juicy
    (3) has been very juicy
    (4) will be very juicy
    (5) would have been very juicy

13. **Sentence 10: Overstuffing a turkey can <u>result in soggy pasty, and</u> undercooked stuffing.**

    Which is the best way to write the underlined portion of the text? If the original is the best way, choose option (1).

    (1) can result in soggy pasty, and
    (2) did result in soggy pasty, and
    (3) has resulted in soggy pasty, and
    (4) can result in soggy, pasty, and
    (5) can result in, soggy, pasty, and

14. **Sentence 11: If you are not using stuffing, you can add some herbs or vegetables to the cavity to improve the flavor of the meet.**

What correction should be made to sentence 11?

(1) remove the comma after *stuffing*
(2) replace *some* with *sum*
(3) insert a comma after *herbs*
(4) replace the first *to* with *too*
(5) replace *meet* with *meat*

15. **Sentence 14:** <u>**Metal or wood are a good**</u> **material for the skewers.**

Which is the best way to write the underlined portion of the text? If the original is the best way, choose option (1).

(1) Metal or wood are a good
(2) Metal or wood were a good
(3) Metal or wood is a good
(4) Metal or wood was a good
(5) Metal or wood will be a good

16. Which revision should be made to paragraph C?

(1) move sentence 12 to the end of paragraph B
(2) move sentence 13 to follow sentence 8
(3) remove sentence 12
(4) remove sentence 10
(5) no revision is necessary

Questions 17–25 refer to the following article.

Watch Out! Someone May Be Reading Your E-Mail!

(A)

(1) The things you produce at work belong to your company, and that includes e-mail messages. (2) Managers may read it at any time, for any reason. (3) They don't even have to get your permission or give you advance notice. (4) In fact, they have the right to show your e-mail to others.

(B)

(5) Obviously, most managers aren't taking the time to read through all of their employees' personal e-mail; its just not worth the effort. (6) However, managers often review e-mail when there are problems with a particular employee or looking for ways to improve customer service. (7) It happens more often than they think. (8) What can you do to protect yourself? (9) Be careful what you write. (10) Don't use e-mail to discuss sensitive matters, like plans to leave your job. (11) When you talk to your doctor do it in person or over the phone. (12) And don't be fooled into thinking you can write anything as long as you deleted the message afterward. (13) In many companies, e-mail is automatically saved without the knowledge of employees. (14) If that's the case at your company, every e-mail message you've ever written may be on file. (15) Even if you've deleted it from your personal records.

17. **Sentence 2: Managers may read it at any time, for any reason.**

    What correction should be made to sentence 2?

    (1) change *Managers* to *manager's*
    (2) change *it* to *them*
    (3) move *at any time* to follow *may*
    (4) start a new sentence with *for any*
    (5) no correction is necessary

18. Which sentence below would be most effective at the beginning of paragraph A?

    (1) Twenty years ago, few people used e-mail.
    (2) Forty-two percent of Americans own computers.
    (3) E-mail makes it a lot easier to keep up with friends and relatives.
    (4) There are more threats to personal privacy today than ever before.
    (5) Most people think that the e-mail they send at work is private, but it isn't.

19. **Sentence 5: Obviously, most managers aren't taking the time to read through all of their employees' personal e-mail; its just not worth the effort.**

What correction should be made to sentence 5?

(1) change *employees'* to *employee's*
(2) change *its* to *it's*
(3) change *their* to *there*
(4) replace *Obviously* with *Being obvious*
(5) no correction is necessary

20. **Sentence 6: However, managers often review e-mail when there are problems with a particular employee <u>or looking</u> for ways to improve customer service.**

Which is the best way to write the underlined portion of the text? If the original is the best way, choose option (1).

(1) or looking
(2) looking
(3) by looking
(4) or look
(5) or when they are looking

21. **Sentence 7: It happens more often than they think.**

Which revision should be made to sentence 7?

(1) replace *happens* with *happened*
(2) change *they* to *them*
(3) change *think* to *thinks*
(4) replace *they* with *people*
(5) no revision is necessary

22. **Sentence 11: When you talk to <u>your doctor do it</u> in person or over the phone.**

Which is the best way to write the underlined portion of the text? If the original is the best way, choose option (1).

(1) your doctor do it
(2) you're doctor do it
(3) your doctor to do it
(4) your doctor doing it
(5) your doctor, do it

23. **Sentence 12: And don't be fooled into thinking you can write anything as long as <u>you deleted</u> the message afterward.**

    Which is the best way to write the underlined portion of the text? If the original is the best way, choose option (1).

    (1) you deleted
    (2) you deletes
    (3) you delete
    (4) your deleting
    (5) you have deleted

24. **Sentences 14 and 15: If that's the case at your company, every e-mail message you've ever written may be on file. Even if you've deleted it from your personal records.**

    The most effective combination of sentences 14 and 15 would include which group of words?

    (1) may be on file, and even if you've deleted it
    (2) may be on file, even if you've deleted it
    (3) may be on file by deleting it
    (4) may be on file to be deleted
    (5) may be on file or deleted

25. Which revision would make this article more effective?

    (1) combine paragraphs A and B
    (2) remove sentence 5
    (3) begin a new paragraph with sentence 8
    (4) remove sentence 12
    (5) begin a new paragraph with sentence 13

Answer Key

CHAPTER 1: The GED Essay

Exercise 1, page 4
1. 45 minutes
2. No. They can answer based upon their lifetime experiences.
3. No. Readers cannot consider these factors in scoring a test.
4. No. The reader may disagree but can only consider the effectiveness of the writing.
5. An essay does not need to contain a certain number of words. It only needs to cover the topic adequately.
6. The minimum passing score for the GED essay test is a 2. If you score below this level, you will have to take both parts of the Language Arts, Writing Test again.

Exercise 2, page 11
Essay 1: This essay most likely scored a 1. The essay really does not develop a main idea about why they are best friends. The essay rambles and lacks relevant details and examples. The number of errors in grammar and spelling interfere with understanding the writer's ideas.

Essay 2: This essay most likely scored a 2. The essay is clear, but there is occasional difficulty understanding the writer's ideas. The essay addresses the prompt, but the focus shifts in the last sentence. The development in the first paragraph consists mainly of a listing of examples of the best friend's work. There is also inconsistent control of grammar and spelling.

Essay 3: This essay most likely scored a 3. The reader generally understands the writer's ideas. The essay has a clear main idea and an organizational plan. The development and examples are mostly relevant to the main idea, and there is good control of the conventions of grammar and spelling.

CHAPTER 2: The Writing Process

Exercise 1, page 17
Sample answers:
1. I think that the perfect number of kids is two.
2. Exercise is important for physical and mental health.
3. Portable communication devices have allowed our society to become more connected.

Exercise 2, page 19
Responses will vary. Share your idea circle with your instructor or another student.

Exercise 3, page 20
Responses will vary. Share your organized idea circle with your instructor or another student.

Exercise 4, page 21
Responses will vary. Share your paragraph with your instructor or another student.

Exercise 5, page 22
Responses will vary. Share your corrections with your instructor or another student.

Exercise 6, page 23
2 Organizing
3 Writing
4 Revising
1 Gathering ideas

Exercise 7, pages 23
1. Gathering ideas
2. Revising
3. Organizing
4. Gathering ideas
5. Organizing
6. Writing
7. Organizing
8. Revising

GED Practice, pages 24–26
Responses will vary. Share your essay with your instructor or another student.

Writing and Life, page 27
Responses will vary. Share your essay with your instructor or another student.

Self-Assessment, page 28
Responses will vary. Share your answers with your instructor or another student.

CHAPTER 3: The One-Paragraph Essay

Exercise 1, pages 30–31
Sample answers:
1. My brother has a beautiful family.
2. My husband and I love to go camping in summer.
3. My favorite pastime is swimming.
4. My family has an important weekly activity: Sunday dinner.

Exercise 2, page 32
Sample answers:
1. They take their kids to Woodland Hills Daycare Center while they are at work.
2. We also get to meet a lot of interesting people.
3. I feel rested and refreshed.
4. After we eat, we visit for two or three hours.

Exercise 3, page 33
1. I am really happy for my brother and his family.
2. When we get home, we feel invigorated and refreshed.
3. After my swim break, I am ready to spend time with my kids.
4. My family and I love our special time together.

Exercise 4, page 33
1. Circle *My favorite free-time activity is going out with my husband.*
2. Seven
3. Sample answer: *When we go out together, we feel as carefree as two teenagers on a date.*
4. Underline *Afterwards, we are relaxed and ready to return to the challenges of our home, our kids, and our jobs.*

Exercise 5, page 35
Part A
Responses will vary. Share your idea list with your instructor or another student.

Part B
Responses will vary. Share your revisions with your instructor or another student.

Exercise 6, page 36
Responses will vary. Share your topic sentence and supporting sentence with your instructor or another student.

Exercise 7, page 37
1. <u>Mary Jane</u> <u>collects</u> model cars and trucks.
2. <u>She</u> <u>has</u> more than 100 models in her collection.
3. <u>She</u> <u>paints</u> all of the models herself.
4. Her most valuable <u>model</u> <u>is</u> a Model T.
5. Her newest <u>model</u> <u>is</u> a PT Cruiser.
6. However, <u>Mary Jane</u> <u>does not own</u> a real car herself.
7. A <u>car</u> <u>is</u> too expensive in the city.

8. So <u>she</u> always <u>takes</u> the bus.
9. <u>She</u> also <u>walks</u> a lot too.
10. Last year <u>she</u> <u>rented</u> a car for her vacation.

Exercise 8, page 38
Part A
1. F
2. S
3. F
4. S
5. S
6. F
7. S
8. F
9. S
10. F

Part B
Sample answers:
1. My favorite pastime is playing basketball.
2. In winter we play at Hill Park Gym.
3. About eight people play every day.
4. I hurt my leg at work, so I have been resting.
5. I can't wait to get back to our games!

Exercise 9, page 39
1. I went to Los Angeles last week to visit my sister Laura and her husband, Vince.
2. We had a lot of fun visiting Disneyland and seeing the ocean.
3. The Pacific Ocean is really beautiful.
4. We went swimming at Santa Monica beach and drove along the coast to Santa Barbara.
5. For New Year's Eve, Laura and Vince are going to visit my husband and me in Chicago.

Exercise 10, page 40
1. My favorite pastime is cooking.
2. I love preparing meals for my family and friends.
3. Of course, I work, so I don't have much time to cook on weekdays.
4. That's too bad!
5. But on weekends I can really enjoy myself in the kitchen.
6. What kinds of things do you make?
7. Well, last weekend, I made fried chicken and mashed potatoes.
8. That sounds delicious!
9. Are pies easy to make?
10. The filling is easy, but the crust is hard.
11. What's in the crust?
12. Flour, shortening, and salt are in the crust.

GED Connection, page 41

1. **(2)** This fragment needs a verb in order to be a complete sentence.
2. **(3)** This is not a question or an exclamation, so it should end with a period.
3. **(3)** Since *Memorial* is part of the name of a specific place, it is a proper noun and should be capitalized.

GED Practice, pages 42–44

Responses will vary. Share your essay with your instructor or another student.

Writing and Life, page 45

Responses will vary. Share your essay with your instructor or another student.

Self-Assessment, page 46

Responses will vary. Share your revisions with your instructor or another student.

CHAPTER 4: Description

Exercise 1, page 48

Sample answers:

1. It is a sleek, speedy sports car.
2. It has special wheels and a paint job that sparkles.
3. The paragraph gives a strong image of the car. An additional detail: It can go from 0 to 60 miles per hour in ten seconds.

Exercise 2, page 49

Circle: 1, 3

Exercise 3, page 50

1. Purrs like a cat; as smooth as butter
2. The upholstery feels as smooth as butter.
3. The hubcaps sparkle in the sun.
4. Scent of a new car
5. Responses will vary.

Exercise 4, page 51

Sample answers:

1. The diamond on Lucille's ring was as big as a golf ball.
2. The sky was a calm, clear blue.
3. In the dark the cat's eyes glowed like hot coals.
4. The waves hit the beach with a terrific spray of white.
5. The car drove quickly and skillfully up the mountain road.

Exercise 5, page 51

Sample answers:

1. The creaky, collapsing house was built in the mid-1800s.
2. I want to buy a car that accelerates rapidly on the highways and flies effortlessly around corners.
3. That man has the most amazing physique I've ever seen, and his eyes are like pools of clear blue water.
4. Would you like an extra-large basket of fries with your double supreme burger and 32-ounce soda?

Exercise 6, page 53

Responses will vary. Share your idea map with your instructor or another student.

Exercise 7, page 54

Responses will vary. Share your revisions with your instructor or another student.

Exercise 8, page 55

Responses will vary. Share your idea map and your revisions with your instructor or another student.

Exercise 9, page 56

1. seems
2. feel *or* are
3. became *or* was
4. seems, sounds, *or* is
5. have become *or* are becoming

Exercise 10, page 57

Sample answers:

1. He served his guests some hot apple pie for dessert.
2. Could you quickly go to the supermarket and get some milk for dinner? It's almost dinnertime.
3. That's a completely wonderful idea!
4. My boss and I get along splendidly.
5. Mrs. Taylor's car is a really ugly color: muted orange.
6. I can hardly understand you. Please talk slowly.
7. I didn't get much sleep during my vacation. The bed in my hotel was very uncomfortable.
8. Drive carefully on your trip to Tennessee.
9. I don't like this cake. It tastes stale.
10. Mr. Applebee drives slowly and carefully.

Exercise 11, page 58

Sample answers:

1. Their vacation in Arizona was full of enjoyable moments and interesting sights.
2. Ms. Espinoza is a thoughtful lady with the disposition of an angel.
3. That rickety farmhouse with the caved-in front porch is aging rapidly.
4. That lazy, pudgy dog is growing larger by the minute.
5. The soup from that crummy restaurant tasted like cold oatmeal.

GED Connection, page 59

1. **(2)** This answer is correct because these words modify *neighbors* and therefore are both adjectives.

2. **(5)** This sentence is correct as written. Choice (1) is not correct because the subject of the sentence, *bus stops,* is plural. Choice (2) is not correct because there are two bus stops, so *stop* must be plural. Choice (3) is not correct because a comma is needed when *and* is used to join two independent clauses. Choice (4) is not correct because the subject of the clause is *market*—a singular noun that requires the singular verb *is.*

3. **(1)** This answer is correct because usually linking verbs such as *taste, smell, feel,* and so on, are in the simple present tense and not the present progressive.

GED Practice, pages 60–62

Responses will vary. Share your one-paragraph descriptive essay with your instructor or another student.

Writing and Life, page 63

Responses will vary. Share your one-paragraph descriptive essay with your instructor or another student.

Self-Assessment, page 64

Responses will vary. Share your revisions with your instructor or another student.

CHAPTER 5: Process

Exercise 1, page 66

1. You need bread, peanut butter, and grape jelly.
2. Six steps are needed to make a PB & J.
3. A PB & J is relatively easy to make.
4. Yes, the paragraph gives a complete set of directions on how to make a PB & J. Some additional information: You can choose a flavor of jelly other than grape.

Exercise 2, page 67

Part A

1. P
2. D
3. P
4. D
5. P

Part B

Circled words should include *how* and *name the steps.*

Exercise 3, pages 68–69

Part A

Sample answers:

1. dog, water, tub, soap or shampoo
2. car, keys
3. clothes, hairbrush, makeup
4. soup, pan, stove

Part B

Responses will vary.

Exercise 4, page 70

a. 4
b. 1
c. 3
d. 6
e. 5
f. 2

Exercise 5, page 72

Responses will vary. Share your flow chart with your instructor or another student.

Exercise 6, page 74

Responses will vary. Share your revisions with your instructor or another student.

Exercise 7, page 74

Responses will vary. Share your flow chart and revisions with your instructor or another student.

Exercise 8, pages 75–76

Part A

Sample answer:

To change the batteries in a smoke detector, **first** get a stepladder and a new battery. **Second,** put the stepladder under the smoke detector and climb up. **Third,** take the cover off the smoke detector. **Fourth,** take out the old battery, and put in the new battery. **Fifth,** put the cover back on the smoke detector. **Sixth,** press the test button to make sure the smoke detector is working. If the detector rings, the alarm is fine. **Next,** climb down the stepladder and put it away. **Last,** throw away the used battery.

Part B

Sample answer:

To change the batteries in a flashlight, first get some new batteries. Then, unscrew the cap of the flashlight, and remove the old batteries. Next, insert the new batteries, and screw the cap back on the flashlight. Turn the flashlight on to make sure it is working. If it lights up, the batteries are working. Last, throw away the old batteries.

Exercise 9, page 77

1. works
2. arrives
3. clocks, goes
4. pack
5. have
6. need
7. gets
8. calls, complains
9. happens, send
10. receives

Exercise 10, page 78

Part A

1. To make a root beer float, put two scoops of ice cream in a tall glass.
2. Then, pour cold root beer over the ice cream.
3. Next, top the ice cream with some whipped cream.
4. Last, put a cherry on top of the float.

Part B

Responses will vary. Share your paragraph with your instructor or another student.

GED Connection, page 79

1. **(5)** This sentence is correct as is.
2. **(4)** The verb *want* has a singular subject, *customer*, so it needs a final *s* in the simple present tense.
3. **(3)** This is the correct placement for the sentence because the employee needs to check the items as he or she puts them in the box before the box is sealed.

GED Practice, pages 80–82

Responses will vary. Share your one-paragraph process essay with your instructor or another student.

Writing and Life, page 83

Responses will vary. Share your one-paragraph process essay with your instructor or another student.

Self-Assessment, page 84

Responses will vary. Share your revisions with your instructor or another student.

CHAPTER 6: The Three-Paragraph Essay

Exercise 1, page 87

The first paragraph is the introductory paragraph, the second paragraph is the body paragraph, and the third paragraph is the concluding paragraph.

Exercise 2, page 88

Part A

1. Exciting sport
2. Requires driving skill
3. Requires mechanical ability

Part B

Yes, the body paragraph contains information about all three phrases.

Part C

Sample answer:

It is a good thesis statement because it gives an accurate idea of the information in the body paragraph.

Exercise 3, page 89

1. a
2. c
3. b

Exercise 4, page 90

1. a. G   b. S
2. a. S   b. G
3. a. G   b. S
4. a. G   b. S
5. a. G   b. S

Exercise 5, page 91

Part A

A: 2

B: 1

C: 3

Part B

Thesis statement: *Listening to blues is my favorite pastime because this music is so expressive and emotional.*

Topic sentence: *Good blues songs express strong feelings about love and life.*

Exercise 6, page 93

1. b
2. a
3. c
4. c
5. b

Exercise 7, page 95

1. Paragraph 1: *Introduction*; Paragraph 2: *Body*; Paragraph 3: *Conclusion*
2. Circle *I love canning because it is a relaxing, old-fashioned pastime that results in plenty of delicious, inexpensive food for my family.*
3. Underline *Canning is an old-fashioned way to relax and prepare good, inexpensive food for my family.*
4. Box *I always look forward to summer so I can do more canning.*

Exercise 8, page 96

1. a
2. b

Exercise 9, page 97

Sample answers:

1. Making hot chocolate is easy.
2. The Grand Canyon is huge.
3. *I Love Lucy* is a really entertaining show.

Exercise 10, page 98

1. Cross off *Do you have a problem with that?* (too informal)
2. Cross off *So get down here!* (too informal)
3. Cross off *Please keep in mind that company policy number 231 states that keys to all company vehicles are to be left in the designated on-site key storage area when the vehicle is parked on company property.* (too formal)

GED Connection, pages 99–100

1. **(2)** This answer is correct because the essay needs a thesis statement. This sentence accurately reflects the main idea of the essay, that PricePlus has a great training program.
2. **(4)** This paragraph needs a topic sentence because it is the body paragraph. This sentence accurately sums up the main idea of the paragraph.
3. **(5)** This option is correct because the sentence is too informal and threatening for the tone of the rest of the essay, which is more formal and professional.

GED Practice, pages 101–103

Responses will vary. Share your three-paragraph essay with your instructor or another student.

Writing and Life, page 103

Responses will vary. Share your essay with your instructor or another student.

Self-Assessment, page 104

Responses will vary. Share your revisions with your instructor or another student.

CHAPTER 7: Cause and Effect

Exercise 1, page 107

Part A

1. Cause: *They got home very late*; effect: *They couldn't find a parking space.*
2. Cause: *He was driving too fast*; effect: *He got into an accident.*
3. Cause: *He got really angry*; effect: *He yelled at the driver of the other car.*
4. Cause: *She wasn't paying attention*; effect: *She ran a red light.*
5. Cause: *He made a wrong turn*; effect: *He got completely lost.*

Part B

Sample answers:

1. He got into an accident.
2. They didn't get enough exercise.
3. She couldn't pay for her groceries.
4. He was in an accident.
5. They swam for two hours.

Exercise 2, page 108

1. Cause; circle *reasons*
2. Cause; circle *why*
3. Cause; circle *why*

Exercise 3, page 110

1. Circle: *why, state reasons*
2. Causes
3. Answers will vary.

Exercise 4, page 111

Answers will vary.

Exercise 5, page 112

Sample answers:

1. He was talking on his cell phone, and he got into an accident.
2. Mr. Williams was driving too quickly, so he got a speeding ticket.
3. She can't drive any more, for her driver's license has expired.

Exercise 6, page 113

Sample answers:

1. He got home late, because he got into an accident.
2. When they received several extra orders, they had to work overtime.
3. We have to get up early tomorrow since our bus leaves at 7:00 A.M.
4. Since the weather was so bad, the train was late.
5. I got a bonus because I worked so hard last month.

Exercise 7, page 115

Part A

1. F
2. C
3. R
4. R
5. F

Part B

Sample answers:

1. Since he didn't have a car, he took the bus.
2. They went to the store because they needed milk and eggs.
3. The car broke down when it ran out of oil.
4. Ms. Pulaski studied every night because she wanted to pass the GED Test.
5. Because he loved his job, he was given a raise.

GED Connection, pages 116–117

1. **(2)** Sentence 2 is a dependent clause, which cannot stand alone. Option (2) joins this dependent clause with sentence 3, an independent clause, to form a complex sentence.

2. **(1)** Sentence 5 is the topic sentence of paragraph B and therefore should go at the beginning of the paragraph.

3. **(5)** The sentences are both independent clauses. Option (5) is the only one that joins them with a comma and a coordinating conjunction. The other options either change the meaning of the sentence or do not make sense.

4. **(3)** Sentence 12 is a run-on. Option (3) correctly joins the two independent clauses with a comma and a coordinating conjunction.

GED Practice, pages 118–120

Responses will vary. Share your cause-and-effect essay with your instructor or another student.

Writing and Life, page 121

Responses will vary. Share your essay with your instructor or another student.

Self-Assessment, page 122

Responses will vary. Share your revisions with your instructor or another student.

CHAPTER 8: Narration

Exercise 1, page 125

1. Description
2. Narration
3. Process
4. Cause and effect
5. Narration
6. Description
7. Cause and effect
8. Process

Exercise 2, page 126

a. 2
b. 4
c. 1
d. 5
e. 3

Exercise 3, page 128

Answers will vary.

Exercise 4, page 129

Answers will vary.

Exercise 5, page 131

1. worked
2. typed
3. prepared
4. did not wash
5. stayed

Exercise 6, page 131

1. got
2. ate
3. read
4. wrote
5. did not go

Exercise 7, page 132

1. was driving
2. was painting; listening *or* was listening
3. were watching
4. was taking
5. was working

Exercise 8, page 133

Part A

Sample answer:

Last weekend we had fun. First, we went swimming at a beautiful beach. The next day, we went to an exciting amusement park. We ate dinner at a fabulous seafood restaurant that night.

Part B

Answers will vary.

Exercise 9, page 134

1. While we were watching the parade, we ate popcorn. (We ate popcorn while we were watching the parade.)

2. After we got up, we got ready to go to Disneyland. (We got ready to go to Disneyland after we got up.)

3. While Kevin and Anthony were playing video games, I sat down and rested. (I sat down and rested while Kevin and Anthony were playing video games.)

4. When Kevin shook hands with Minnie Mouse, I took his picture. (I took his picture when Kevin shook hands with Minnie Mouse.)

GED Connection, page 135

1. **(3)** The original sentence is a comma splice. Option (3) uses a subordinating conjunction to join the clauses.

2. **(5)** This subordinating conjunction shows the correct order of the events: First they looked at the gift shop, and then they left the museum.

3. **(1)** This phrase shows the chronological order of events: They left the museum and went to the restaurant.

GED Practice, pages 136–137
Responses will vary. Share your narrative essay with your instructor or another student.

Writing and Life, page 137
Responses will vary. Share your essay with your instructor or another student.

Self-Assessment, page 138
Responses will vary. Share your revisions with your instructor or another student.

CHAPTER 9: Comparison and Contrast

Exercise 1, page 141
Part A
1. Comparison
2. Contrast
3. Comparison
4. Contrast
5. Contrast

Part B
Answers will vary.

Exercise 2, page 142
1. Circle *rather*; yes
2. No
3. Circle *better*; yes
4. Circle *advantages and disadvantages*; yes
5. Circle *better*; yes

Exercise 3, page 144

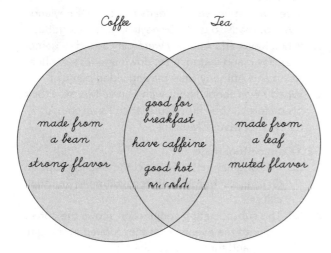

Exercise 4, page 145
Answers will vary.

Exercise 5, page 146
Answers will vary.

Exercise 6, page 147
1. Hurt in a fall, the skier returned to the lodge.
2. Crying and unhappy, she told the doctor what happened.
3. In a calm voice, the doctor told her that her injuries were not serious.
4. Concerned for her health, he helped her to their room to get some rest.

Exercise 7, page 148
1. With a smile, he gave me my change.
2. Running quickly, the dog barked at the car.
3. Badly hurt in the car crash, Mr. Maguire arrived at the hospital in an ambulance.
4. They couldn't find the flashlight under the sofa.
5. Searching frantically around the neighborhood, the woman finally found her missing dog.

Exercise 8, page 149
Sample answers:
1. Since he was reading the newspaper, time passed quickly.
2. Closing the door, he locked the keys in the room.
3. Since he was stuck in traffic, the meeting started without him.
4. As you enter the supermarket, the produce is on the left.
5. The furniture was admired as the guests entered the room.

Exercise 9, page 150
1. Frank Ramirez, the president of the company, made the announcement.
2. Maui, a beautiful island, is part of the Hawaiian Islands.
3. My neighbor, Miss Appleby, is really nice.
4. Lake Michigan, one of the Great Lakes, is one of the largest bodies of water in North America.
5. Bert Bowden, a retired bus driver, is taking the GED Test this year.

GED Connection, pages 151–152
1. **(2)** The original sentence contains a dangling modifier. Option (1) gives the modifier a clear reference.
2. **(2)** The phrase *his family's favorite pizza restaurant*, is an appositive, which must be set off by commas.
3. **(1)** The verbal phrase *sitting on the dining room table* is a misplaced modifier. It needs to be moved closer to the word it modifies—*salad*.
4. **(4)** The phrase *with the correct address* is a dangling modifier. Option (4) changes the phrase into a dependant clause.

GED Practice, pages 153–155
Responses will vary. Share your comparison-contrast essay with your instructor or another student.

Writing and Life, page 155
Responses will vary. Share your essay with your instructor or another student.

Self-Assessment, page 156
Responses will vary. Share your revisions with your instructor or another student.

CHAPTER 10: The Five-Paragraph Essay

Exercise 1, page 159
a. The first paragraph
b. *There were lost of interesting activities all three days of the reunion.*
c. The second paragraph
d. The third paragraph
e. The fourth paragraph
f. *The reunion began with a fun dinner Friday evening.*
g. *On Saturday we spent the entire day together.*
h. *On Sunday we had a family picnic in the park.*
i. The fifth paragraph

Exercise 2, page 160
Circle 1, 3, 5, and 7.

Exercise 3, page 160
Sample answers:
1. My favorite way to spend a rainy Sunday afternoon is to read a book, bake cookies, or rent a movie.
2. People shouldn't smoke because it is expensive, disgusting, and unhealthful.

Exercise 4, page 161
Sample answers:
1. Thesis statement: *There are three reasons I prefer to live in the city instead of in a small town.*

   Topic sentence 1: *Everything you need is within walking distance in the city.*

   Topic sentence 2: *You are surrounded by art and culture in the city.*

   Topic sentence 3: *It is easy to get around via public transportation in the city.*
2. Thesis statement: *A good citizen should stay informed, vote, and participate in community projects.*

   Topic sentence 1: *A good citizen should stay informed about what is going on in his/her city.*

   Topic sentence 2: *A good citizen should make a point to vote in every city election.*

   Topic sentence 3: *A good citizen should give back to the community by participating in community projects.*

Exercise 5, page 163
Sample answer:
   Imagine you've just sent your husband to the grocery store to pick up some butter and eggs for a cake you are making. Suddenly you realize that you also need some milk. What do you do? A mere decade ago, you would have to wait for him to return and send him out again. Today, however, you simply pick up the phone and call your husband on his cell phone. Inventions such as the cell phone, pagers, and e-mail have helped us to communicate more efficiently than we did 10 years ago. Technology allows us to stay in contact anywhere, at any time, and in a variety of ways.

Exercise 6, page 165
1. b, f, g
2. a, d
3. c, e, h

Exercise 7, page 166
Part A
a. 2
b. 1
c. 4
d. 5
e. 3

Part B
1. This essay is an example of a process essay.
2. Underline *The three basic steps are easy—mixing the ingredients, letting the dough rise, and baking the bread.*
3. Circle *Mixing the ingredients is the first step; The second step, letting the dough rise, is the easiest; and The third step, baking the bread, happens after the dough has risen a second time.*

Exercise 8, page 167
Begin a new paragraph with the sentence *Williamson Decorating can also redo your bathroom.*

Exercise 9, page 169
Paragraphs A and B should be combined.

Exercise 10, page 170
1. Cross off: *They had fun before school let out, too, going on a Boy Scout camping trip in May.*
2. Cross off: *My other best friend, Marty, isn't as lucky as Stephen.*

GED Connection, pages 171–172
1. **(1)** Sentence 13 belongs at the end of paragraph B because it is about the main idea of paragraph B—knowing your goals.
2. **(4)** Sentences 18–23 are about one main idea mentioned in the thesis statement—using a to-do list. Therefore these sentences should all be in a single paragraph of their own that begins with sentence 18.

3. **(5)** Sentence 23 is about keeping a record of expenses, which has nothing to do with the thesis statement—ways to avoid procrastination. This sentence should be removed from the paragraph.

GED Practice, pages 173–174
Responses will vary. Share your five-paragraph essay with your instructor or another student.

Writing and Life, page 175
Responses will vary. Share your essay with your instructor or another student.

Self-Assessment, page 176
Responses will vary. Share your revisions with your instructor or another student.

CHAPTER 11: Persuasion

Exercise 1, page 179
Circle 1, 3, 6, 9, and 10.

Exercise 2, page 180
1. b
2. b
3. a
4. b

Exercise 3, page 181
Sample answers:
1. The old school building is overcrowded and dangerous.
2. Traffic downtown would be reduced.
3. A diet rich in fruit and vegetables helps lower cholesterol.
4. Wearing a seatbelt can mean the difference between life and death.
5. Recycling helps conserve valuable natural resources.

Exercise 4, page 181
1. The first paragraph is the introduction; the second, third, and fourth paragraphs are body paragraphs 1, 2, and 3; the fifth paragraph is the conclusion.
2. Circle *Smoking makes people unattractive; Cigarette smoking is also expensive;* and *Most important, cigarette smoking is terrible for people's health.*
3. Underline *People should stop smoking immediately because it's unattractive, expensive, and dangerous.*

Exercise 5, page 184
A. Introduction
B. Good for your health
   1. **Running burns calories**
   2. **Running lowers blood pressure and cholesterol**
C. Relaxing

   1. **Running gets your mind off your problems**
   2. **Running lets you have some fun**
D. Contact with nature
   1. **You can run in parks, along the beach, or in forest preserves**
   2. **You can see birds, trees, and squirrels**
E. Conclusion

Exercise 6, page 185
Answers for Parts A and B will vary.

Exercise 7, page 186
Answers will vary.

Exercise 8, page 187
Circle *because, Since, If,* and *because*

Exercise 9, page 188
1. If people stop smoking now, they will save a lot of money.
2. He started getting more exercise because he needed to lower his blood pressure.
3. Mary Beth joined a gym so that she could use the weight machines.
4. Jayson stopped eating potato chips since they are high in fat.
5. Roberta may get cancer unless she stops smoking.

Exercise 10, page 189
1. Mark spoke to Bill, and then Bill *(or Mark)* called Marisa.
2. The city organized music festivals and art fairs so that tourists would come from all over to visit.
3. Maria doesn't know Ana, but Ana *(or Maria)* knows Chen.
4. I bought ice cream cones for my nephews Ricky and Billy, but Ricky *(or Billy)* didn't eat his.
5. Government officials want to raise rich people's taxes.

Exercise 11, page 190
1. He stopped smoking and eating fatty foods.
2. Mrs. Barnes is nervous, insecure, and disrespectful.
3. The waitress, took our order, brought us our drinks, but forgot to bring us our sandwiches.
4. My favorite hobbies are running, going to the movies, and reading.

GED Connection, pages 191–192
1. **(4)** This option makes the connected elements parallel—*get, cut down,* and *develop.*
2. **(2)** This option uses the subordinating conjunction *so that* to join the clauses to form a complex sentence.
3. **(1)** This option replaces the unclear pronoun they with a clear noun—*employees.*
4. **(5)** This option makes the connected elements parallel—*weight rooms, indoor tracks, lap pools,* and *basketball courts.*

GED Practice, pages 193–194
Responses will vary. Share your persuasive essay with your instructor or another student.

Writing and Life, page 195
Responses will vary. Share your essay with your instructor or another student.

Self-Assessment, page 196
Responses will vary. Share your revisions with your instructor or another student.

CHAPTER 12: Improving Your Writing

Exercise 1, page 202
1. c
2. a
3. b
4. e
5. d

Exercise 2, page 202
Part A
This essay would probably receive a 2. It responds to the prompt but goes off topic in the paragraph about the cost of shelter. It has good organization but is missing a concluding paragraph. It also lacks plenty of examples. The first two body paragraphs each only have one specific example about the cost of food and clothing. There are a few errors in Edited American English, and the word choice is rather repetitive, such as the repetition of the words *go up* and *worry*.

Part B
The writer should probably pay attention to organization, development and details, and word choice.

Exercise 3, page 204
Part A
When scored by actual GED readers, this essay received a 2. It addresses the prompt and immediately establishes a main idea. However, the long paragraph shows little planning or organization and makes it difficult to follow the writer's ideas. The writer's focus on changing his or her attitude toward other people and life shifts at one point toward a discussion of life as a game. Other than the game metaphor, idea development is limited to a repetition of the need to change attitudes. Sentences that run together make reading difficult, and there is noticeable repetition of phrases. There are also few errors in Edited American English, but the absence of appropriate commas makes the essay hard to read. Word choices are frequently inappropriate—the tone varies between slang and conventional writing.

Exercise 4, page 207
Answers will vary.

Exercise 5, page 208
Answers will vary.

GED Practice, pages 209–211
Responses will vary. Share your essay with your instructor or another student.

Writing and Life, page 211
Responses will vary. Share your essay with your instructor or another student.

Self-Assessment, page 212
Responses will vary. Share your revisions with your instructor or another student.

CHAPTER 13: Review

Exercise 1, page 215
1. One paragraph, three-paragraph, and five-paragraph essay
2. Three-paragraph, and five-paragraph essay
3. One paragraph, three paragraph, and five paragraph essay
4. Three-paragraph and five-paragraph essay
5. Three-paragraph and five-paragraph essay
6. Five-paragraph essay

Exercise 2, page 215
a. 3
b. 1
c. 2
d. 5
e. 4

Exercise 3, page 217
1. Descriptive writing
2. Process writing
3. Cause-and-effect writing
4. Narrative writing
5. Comparitive/contrastive writing
6. Persuasive writing

Exercise 4, page 218
1. d
2. c
3. e
4. f
5. a
6. b

Exercise 5, page 223
First circle: Steps 1-4 (Mixing the batter)
Second circle: Steps 5 to 8 (Baking the cornbread)
Third circle: Steps 9 to 11 (Serving the cornbread)

GED Practice, pages 224–225
Responses will vary. Share your essay with your instructor or another student.

Writing and Life, page 225
Responses will vary. Share your essay with your instructor or another student.

Self-Assessment, page 226
Responses will vary. Share your revisions with your instructor or another student.

CHAPTER 14: Taking the Test

GED Practice, pages 230–231
Responses will vary. Share your essay with your instructor or another student.

Writing and Life, page 232
Responses will vary. Share your essay with your instructor or another student.

Self-Assessment, page 232
Responses will vary. Share your revisions with your instructor or another student.

Writing Handbook

GED Connection, pages 259–268

1. **(4)** The subject of the sentence is singular—*one*. The correct verb is *has* not *have*.
2. **(2)** This answer shows the best way to rewrite the original sentence while eliminating the repetition of the word *reports*.
3. **(4)** *Coretech* is a proper noun and must be capitalized.
4. **(5)** Paragraph B is about precautions that will take place in the immediate future. The past tense *was set* needs to be replaced with the future tense *will be*.
5. **(1)** This answer effectively combines the two sentences while maintaining the same meaning as the original sentences.
6. **(3)** This sentence addresses all the supporting sentences in the paragraph. The other sentences are too specific to be the topic sentence or do not relate to the other sentences in the paragraph.
7. **(2)** The antecedent in this sentence is *mail*, which is singular. The singular pronoun and verb *it is* should be used instead of the plural *they are*.

8. **(3)** This sentence contains a dangling modifier. Changing the modifier to a dependent clause corrects the error.
9. **(5)** This revision places the verbs in parallel structure—*continue* and *revise*.
10. **(2)** The homonym *it's*, meaning *it is*, makes sense in this sentence—*It is holiday time*.
11. **(1)** This revision places all three verbs in parallel structure—*preheat*, *take*, and *remove*.
12. **(2)** The rest of paragraph B is written in the present tense, so sentence 7 should contain the present tense verb *is*.
13. **(4)** This option correctly places a comma between the items in a series—*soggy, pasty*, and *undercooked*.
14. **(5)** The homonym *meat* makes more sense here.
15. **(3)** A compound subject with *or* uses the singular form of the verb—*is*.
16. **(3)** Sentence 12 is about gravy and does not belong in a paragraph about cooking a turkey.
17. **(2)** The pronoun *it* is a substitute for *e-mail messages*, which is plural. The plural pronoun *them* should be used.
18. **(5)** This sentence would be a great topic sentence for the article. It grabs the reader's interest by pointing out that something he or she probably believes really isn't true.
19. **(2)** The homonym *it's*, meaning *it is*, makes sense in this sentence—*it is just not worth the effort*.
20. **(5)** The verbs in the original sentence are not in parallel structure. This sentence corrects the error.
21. **(4)** *They* is a vague pronoun in this sentence. *People* is a more specific word.
22. **(5)** A comma must separate the clauses in a complex sentence when the dependent clause precedes the independent clause.
23. **(3)** You cannot write a message in the present and delete it in the past. *Deleted* should be changed to *delete* so it is in the same tense as *can write*.
24. **(2)** The original sentence 15 is a fragment. Adding it to sentence 14 corrects the error.
25. **(3)** Sentences 5–7 are about why and when managers read e-mail. Sentences 8–14 are about how to protect your privacy. The two sections break nicely into different paragraphs.

Evaluation Chart

This book helped you prepare for Part II of the Language Arts, Writing Test—the Essay. However, the essay counts toward only 37 to 40 percent of your total score. Are you ready for Part I of the Language Arts, Writing Test? On the following chart, circle the number of any item you answered incorrectly in the GED Connection exercise on pages 259–268. Pay particular attention to areas where you missed half or more of the questions. For those questions that you missed, review the skill pages indicated. These pages can be found in other texts in Contemporary's GED Program.

Skill Area	Item Number	Review pages in *Contemporary's GED Language Arts, Writing*	Review pages in *Contemporary's Complete GED*
ORGANIZATION			
Text divisions	25	120–126	157–160
Topic sentences	6, 18	115–119	153–157
Unity/coherence	16	127–133	160–165
SENTENCE STRUCTURE			
Complete sentences, fragments, and sentence combining	5, 24	19–24, 83–104	105–108, 110–112
Run-on sentences/comma splices		86–88, 96	108–109
Wordiness/repetition	2	97–98, 103–104	116–121
Coordination/subordination		83–84, 89–98	116–118
Modification	8	145–153	126–128
Parallelism	9, 11, 20	154–156	129–134
USAGE			
Subject-verb agreement	1, 15	51–59, 62–73	87–91
Verb tense/form	4, 12, 23	51–61, 101–102	73–86
Pronoun reference/antecedent agreement	7, 17, 21	38–42, 157–165	91–95
MECHANICS			
Capitalization	3	29, 34–35, 177–178	135–138
Punctuation (commas)	13, 22	31, 87, 93, 96, 183–185	139–144
Spelling (possessives, contractions, and homonyms)	10, 14, 19	43, 179–182	147–149

Glossary

A

adjective

a word that describes a noun or pronoun.

The <u>talented</u> actress walked up to the podium to accept her Academy Award.

adverb

a word that describes a verb.

The getaway car sped <u>quickly</u> down the highway.

adverb of sequence

a word such as *first, last, then, after that, next,* or *last* that indicates the order of an action in relation to other actions.

adverb of time

a word such as *yesterday* or *last week* that is used to indicate when an action occurred.

antecedent

the word or words that a pronoun refers to in a sentence.

<u>Emily and Bill</u> went shopping to buy an anniversary present for their parents.

appositive

a noun phrase that gives more information about a noun or pronoun in a sentence; an appositive must be set off from the rest of the sentence with commas.

My dog, <u>Abby,</u> is a faithful companion.

B

body paragraph

the paragraph that develops a particular detail of the thesis statement; a three-paragraph essay contains one body paragraph while a five-paragraph essay contains three.

brainstorming

a technique used to gather ideas, in which the writer lists ideas as they come to him or her.

C

cause	an event that makes something happen.
cause-and-effect-writing	a style of writing that explains the causes or effects of a particular action or event.

She ran a red light because she wasn't paying attention.

chronological order	a pattern of organization that lists ideas in the order in which they occurred.
clause	a group of words with a subject and a verb that is part of a larger sentence.

I am flying to Tokyo tomorrow, but my husband is flying to Mexico City.

comma splice	a sentence consisting of two clauses joined by a comma without a conjunction.

Erin went to the hospital, she was in labor.

comparative writing	a style of writing that allows the writer to find similarities between two things.

Cats and dogs are popular pets.

complete sentence	a sentence that contains a subject and a verb.

My mother baby-sits for us.
SUBJECT   VERB

complex sentence	a sentence that contains a dependent clause connected to an independent clause.

Joe and Felicia bought the couch while it was still on sale.

compound sentence	a sentence that contains two independent clauses joined with a coordinating conjunction.

Regina is going to a local college, but her sister is going to college in another state.

concluding paragraph	the final paragraph in a multi-paragraph essay; the concluding paragraph summarizes the essay and relates the main idea to broader issues.
contrastive writing	a style of writing that allows the writer to find differences between two things.

Cats are quiet, but dogs are often noisy.

coordinating conjunction	a word used to connect independent clauses in a compound sentence.

Regina is going to a local college, but her sister is going to college in another state.

D

dangling modifier   a word or phrase that has no word to describe in a sentence.

Typing furiously, the paper was finished just in time for class.

dependent clause   a clause that depends on another clause in order to make sense; a dependent clause makes up part of a complex sentence.

Joe and Felicia bought the couch while it was still on sale.

descriptive writing   a style of writing that tells the reader what a person, place, or thing is like.

My car is a sturdy sport-utility vehicle.

E

effect   the result of something that happened first.

essay diagram   a writing tool that helps the writer visualize the structure of an essay.

exclamation   a sentence that shows great interest or emotion; an exclamation always ends with an exclamation point.

What a great performance!

F

five-paragraph essay   an essay that consists of an introductory paragraph, three body paragraphs, and a concluding paragraph.

flow chart   a graphic organizer that consists of a series of boxes and arrows; ideas are placed in the boxes in the correct order.

fragment   a group of words that does not fulfill the requirements of a complete sentence; a dependent clause that stands alone.

Hoping I would pass the test.

G

gathering ideas   the first step in the writing process, in which the writer figures out the main idea of the essay and thinks of supporting details.

I

idea circle	a writing tool used to gather ideas; the main idea goes in the circle and supporting ideas are written on spokes coming from the center of the circle.
idea list	a writing tool used to gather ideas; the main idea is written at the top of the list, followed by a list of supporting ideas.
idea map	a writing tool used to gather ideas; a writer arranges ideas on an idea map to show how they relate to the main idea of an essay.
imperative	a sentence that tells someone to do something; the subject of a command is always understood to be *you*.

> Go upstairs to your room now!

independent clause	a clause that can stand alone as a complete sentence; two independent clauses are joined to create a compound sentence.

> <u>Regina is going to a local college</u>, but <u>her sister is going to college in another state.</u>

indent	to begin the first word of a paragraph a few spaces to the right of the margin.
introductory paragraph	the first paragraph in a multi-paragraph essay; the introductory paragraph builds the reader's interest and states the main idea.

L

linking verb	a verb that links the subject of a sentence to words that describe or rename it.

> That child <u>is</u> sick.

M

main idea	the point of view that an essay discusses or develops.
misplaced modifier	a modifier that is not placed near the word it modifies in a sentence.

> <u>Driving over a curb</u>, the car hit a tree.

N

narrative writing	a style of writing that tells about something that happened in the past.

> I was queen of the Barnum & Bailey Circus when I was five years old.

O

one-paragraph essay	an essay that consists of a single paragraph with a topic sentence, a number of supporting sentences, and a concluding sentence.
order of importance	a pattern of organization that lists ideas from least to most important.
organizing	the second step in the writing process, in which the writer makes sure there are enough supporting details, ensures that the details are all about the main idea, and puts ideas in an order that makes sense.
outline	a writing tool used to organize information into points and subpoints.

P

parallel structure	a correct form of sentence structure in which all elements of a compound sentence have the same form. The runner <u>stretched</u> out her muscles, <u>ran</u> a warm-up lap, and <u>took</u> her place at the starting line.
past continuing tense	a verb tense used to show a past action that continued for some time. We <u>were studying</u> for the GED Test.
persuasive writing	a style of writing that is used to convince the reader to believe in something or to do something. Live the good life—move to Texas!
prepositional phrase	a word group that starts with a preposition and ends with a noun or pronoun; a prepositional phrase describes another word in the sentence. The Elliott family just bought a house <u>on a lake</u>.
process writing	a style of writing that tells the reader how to do something. To get to the conference room, walk down the hallway and go through the second door on your left.
proper adjective	an adjective formed from a proper noun; a proper adjective is generally capitalized. She loves to eat <u>Mexican</u> food.
proper noun	a noun that names a specific person, place or thing; a proper noun is generally capitalized. <u>Ralph</u> and his daughter are going to look at colleges in <u>California</u>.

R

revising
the fourth and final step in the writing process, in which a writer reviews and corrects an essay.

run-on sentence
a sentence consisting of two or more clauses that are not joined with a conjunction.

> Jerry went to the grocery store I went home.

S

sequence word
a word such as *first, second, next,* and *last* that helps the reader to understand the order of steps or events in a paragraph.

simple past tense
a verb tense used to show an action that occurred at a specified time in the past.

> Last year, I <u>decided</u> to get my GED.

simple present tense
a verb tense used to show a habitual or regular action.

> She <u>walks</u> her dog every day.

subject
the part of a sentence that tells the reader who or what the sentence is about.

> <u>The blue dress</u> looks nice on you.

subordinating conjunction
a word that joins a dependent clause to an independent clause.

> Joe and Felicia bought the couch <u>while</u> it was still on sale.

supporting sentence
a sentence in a paragraph that gives more information about the main idea presented in the topic sentence.

T

T-chart
a tool for gathering ideas for a cause-and-effect essay; causes are listed in the first column and effects are listed in the second column.

thesis statement
a sentence that states the main idea of the essay and indicates the type of information that will be contained in the body paragraphs; the thesis statement is usually the last sentence in the introductory paragraph.

three-paragraph essay
an essay that consists of an introductory paragraph, a body paragraph, and a concluding paragraph.

tone
the style in which a sentence or paragraph is written.

topic sentence
a sentence in a paragraph that states the main idea of the paragraph.

V

Venn diagram   a writing tool used to gather information for a comparison-contrast essay; a Venn diagram consists of two linked circles with similarities listed where the circles overlap and differences listed where the circles are separate.

verb   the word in a sentence that tells what the subject is or does.

The employees <u>entered</u> the conference room.

verbal phrase   a modifying phrase that uses a verb form to describe a noun.

Swinging her long hair from side to side, the girl skipped down the street.

W

writing   the third step in the writing process in which the writer uses an organized idea list to write an essay.

writing process   a four-step plan for writing an essay.

Index